MASQUERADE

The Visitor's Introduction to Trinidad and Tobago

Jeremy Taylor

with photographs by
Mark Lyndersay

Dear Jack,

A souvenir of a fleeting
visit to Trinidad & Tobago
10ᵗʰ – 12ᵗʰ June, 1988

From Anne & Jerry Sanche

M

First published 1986

Published by *Macmillan Publishers Ltd*
London and Basingstoke
Associated companies and representatives in Accra,
Auckland, Delhi, Dublin, Gaborone, Hamburg, Harare,
Hong Kong, Kuala Lumpur, Lagos, Manzini, Melbourne,
Mexico City, Nairobi, New York, Singapore, Tokyo

ISBN 0-333-41985-5

Printed in Hong Kong

British Library Cataloguing in Publication Data
Taylor, Jeremy
    Masquerade: the visitor's introduction to
    Trinidad and Tobago.
    1. Trinidad and Tobago—Description and travel
    —Guide-books
    I. Title
    917.298′3044   F2122

ISBN 0-333-41985-5

Contents

Acknowledgements

Wittingly or not, many people helped me write this book and saved it from some of its errors. Among them are my wife Gretta, Pat Bishop, Angela Hamel-Smith, Michael Anthony, Joan Massiah, Elizabeth Crouch, Bill Lennox, Esla Morris and Lennie Yates, Mark Lyndersay, Professor J.S. Kenny, Dr Carol James and the staff of the Wildlife Office of the Forestry Department. To all of these, and to others unnamed, my thanks.

As well-informed readers will readily observe, the influence of the specialists is often inescapable, and I would like to acknowledge a particular debt to Dr Bridget Brereton's *A History of Modern Trinidad 1783–1962*, Errol Hill's *The Trinidad Carnival*, and John Newel Lewis's *Ajoupa*.

Certain sections of this book first appeared in earlier versions in the London *Times*, *BWIA Sunjet* and *Tempo*.

J.T.

Additional photographic material has been provided by Bill Lennox (pages 19, 27, 35, 55, 75, 87, 90, 94, 107, 110 and 122) and Michael Bourne (pages 30, 106, 111, 114 and 118).

1

Introductions

A few hours out from London, as the plane began to sniff the warm air of the Caribbean, the people on board – many of them going home for Carnival – began to change identity. Some slunk quietly into the toilets and re-emerged shorn of sweaters, jackets and ties. Others discarded their Heathrow newspapers and began to stretch and flirt with the flight attendants. The burly man in front of me, who for some hundreds of miles had been studying *The Economist*, appeared grinning over the back of the seat. 'Hi!' he said to an English girl nearby. 'Yuh playin' mas'? Who yuh playin' with?'

It was the inescapable Carnival question: how are you spending your Carnival? She was shy but game, a young reporter going out to write about the Carnival – the masquerade, the mas'. She hadn't signed up with anybody's band, she said; should she? The man looked at her in mock horror, arms theatrically spread. 'Yuh makin' joke!' he said. 'Not playin' mas'? Yuh mad or what? Yuh don't know Trinidad have the sweetest masquerade in the world? That it make Rio look stupid? What happen to you, girl? But yuh bound to get a costume, all right? Don't worry about that.' He slapped heavily beringed hands on the back of the seat and subsided, rolling up his sleeves. 'Trinidad and Tobago,' he said to the plane. 'Carnival. *That* is mas'.'

The Islands

Later on, it's Tobago that appears first: a fleeting image of green hills and white beaches far below the cabin window as the plane eases down from the north. Then, suddenly, you're over Trinidad's north coast, the wildest and loveliest part of the island; those green

The thickly forested hills of the Northern Range stretch along Trinidad's north coast

forested hills, rising to just over 3,000 feet, are really an extension of Venezuela, an arm of the distant Andes stretching along the northern coast of South America and into Trinidad. As the plane banks for its final approach to Piarco airport, the urban sprawl of Port of Spain erupts on the left, its suburbs mushrooming along the foothills, while on the right are the flat green plains of Caroni, stubbled with sugar. Beside them stretches the Gulf of Paria, almost enclosed between Trinidad and mainland Venezuela.

Below, crowded highways and empty brown tracks slice through the green sugar fields. The orange flame of gas flares from the oil-belt refineries on the Gulf coast; oil tankers nose through the waters of the Gulf – signs that Trinidad and Tobago no longer depends on sugar. And just out of sight over the southern horizon, beyond the smaller hills in the centre and south of the island, lies the narrow channel between Trinidad and the South American mainland through which, almost five centuries ago, Christopher Columbus sailed swiftly on the current, praising the Holy Trinity for a sight of land after a long and difficult third voyage to the new world, and calling the island La Trinidad.

Tobago and Trinidad are the most southerly of the Caribbean islands; they are *in* the Caribbean all right, yet sometimes seem to be on the fringes of it – one eye turned northwards towards the islands, the other turned south towards the South American continent of which both islands were once part.

It's an ambivalence that shows through in many subtle ways. Trinidad and Tobago is perceived by the rest of the Caribbean as a law unto itself – generous and Caribbean-spirited, but quite capable of going its own way. It was the one island state in the Caribbean that remained aloof and disapproving when American forces invaded Grenada in 1983. Twenty years earlier, it was Trinidad and Tobago's decision that finally put paid to the quivering corpse of West Indian federation after Jamaica had dealt it its death blow in 1962: the Prime Minister of the time, Dr Eric Williams, in a famous mathematical calculation based on Jamaica's secession from the 10-member group, announced 'One from ten leaves nought' and prepared for independence alone.

Trinidad and Tobago has far and away the most lavish natural resources in the Caribbean archipelago, in the shape of plentiful oil and even more plentiful natural gas; its oil boom of the 1970's and early 1980's again set it apart from most of its Caribbean neighbours. And somehow the country refuses to conform with the stock Caribbean images. It has never till now shown much serious interest in large-scale tourism; it has moved well ahead of its neighbours in the industrialisation process, producing steel, methanol, urea and ammonia (by 1984 it was the world's second largest ammonia exporter after the USSR).

Although you can easily find the straw-hatted minstrel strumming *Yellow Bird* or *Island in the Sun*, Trinidad and Tobago has

The Caribbean

given the world a good deal more than the lethargic stereotypes of Caribbean entertainment: it has produced novelist V. S. Naipaul, the late great Winifred Atwell, Angostura bitters, the most congenial of the world's great Carnivals, a wholly original musical instrument fashioned out of industrial waste (the steel pan), and a song form (calypso) with a wholly distinctive rhythm, in which the singer has more licence than the leader writer of the *Washington Post* to comment on the personalities and trends of the day.

Because of its continental past, Trinidad and Tobago has an abundance of natural life crowded into a fairly small land area (1,864 and 116 square miles respectively), which ranges in a few miles from mountains to plains, from beaches to swamps and savannahs; there are over 400 species of birds, more than 600 species of butterflies, and consequently several species of naturalists swarming most of the year.

The two islands make a neat, contrasting pair. Trinidad claims the excitement and activity, the entertainment, the sights, the pace, the noise, the traffic jams. Tobago offers the best beaches, tranquillity, relaxation; it has the beachfront hotels, the calm blue waters and white sand, the slower pace. In Tobago, you unwind after Trinidad – Trinidadians themselves are Tobago's most frequent visitors, using the sister island largely as a weekend and holiday resort.

The two islands have had very different histories, though. They were joined as a single state by the British only at the end of the 19th century, when Tobago's economy collapsed and London could think of nothing to do with the island except tack it onto nearby Trinidad. By that time, Tobago – whose name is probably linked to tobacco, which its first Amerindian settlers grew there – had suffered a classic Caribbean colonial history, changing hands 31 times between the Dutch, the French, the Spanish and the English as the European naval powers struggled for control of the Caribbean. More peaceably, it may just have been the island which Daniel Defoe had in mind when, thousands of miles away, he looked for a suitable setting for his fictional castaway Robinson Crusoe – at least, Tobagonians like to think so.

By the beginning of the 19th century, Tobago had settled down as a British slave colony; but Trinidad was only just coming to life, and there the British were newcomers. For the Spanish, who had held Trinidad more or less undisturbed since Columbus came and

5

went in 1498, the island had been merely a staging post on their fruitless journeys into South America in search of El Dorado, the mythical kingdom of gold. They did nothing to develop the island until the 1780's, when they engineered an influx of French settlers to provide it with a population. Trinidad's development thus began late and progressed fast; after the English seized the island in 1797, it found itself with Spanish laws and an English governor but more or less run by the French. Trinidad had a comparatively brief period of serious slavery, a half century or so, before abolition in 1834; many of the islands to the north suffered for two or three hundred years.

The People

That unusual past explains Trinidad and Tobago's very mixed population. Its first people were Amerindian, part of the great migration that populated the Americas over the centuries, one arm of which moved along the northern coast of South America and up the Caribbean island chain. These were the people Columbus encountered in 1498, and they lasted longer in Trinidad than in the other islands because the Spanish lacked the energy and the resources to enslave them effectively.

But little remains of the Amerindian civilisation now, apart from a few pockets of remote descendants mainly in north central Trinidad. The Spanish, French and British more or less coexisted in Trinidad, rather than throwing each other out as they tended to do elsewhere. All three used African slaves, imported either directly or from other parts of the Caribbean, so that today 40–45 per cent of Trinidad and Tobago's 1.1 million population is of African descent, though from a much wider than usual range of tribal roots.

After abolition, the British chose Trinidad as the laboratory for bizarre experiments in alternative labour in order to keep the sugar estates alive and growing. From 1845 there was a large flow of imported labour from India, with the result that another 40–45 per cent (and probably a slight majority) of the modern population is of Indian descent. Labour was seduced or coerced from other parts of the world too, so that Trinidad and Tobago has communities with their roots in China, the Middle East, Portugal, Madeira and Corsica and other parts of the Mediterranean. Most of these groups have retained something of their ethnic identity while at the same time assuming a shared Trinidadian one. The Indians, who often arrived in family units and were allowed to acquire land, retained much more of their cultural traditions than the Africans, whose families were separated and who, as slaves, remained landless.

The mingling of these widely different traditions has produced a population that is unusually mixed and which contains very striking physical beauty; the inevitable underlying tensions have been successfully contained and are becoming steadily less important. Traditional divisions of activity (Whites and Indians in business, Africans in the public service; Indians in opposition, Africans in government) are fading.

Politics

Trinidad and Tobago has enjoyed substantial social and political stability since it became independent from Britain in 1962. Politically, the first three decades after self-government were dominated by a single political party – the pragmatic and essentially conservative People's National Movement (PNM), which came to power in

The Red House in Port of Spain: meeting place for the two houses of Parliament

1956 soon after it was founded by that fiery intellectual Dr Eric Williams, and stayed there. The PNM found its strongest roots in the African, largely urban population where the majority of the constituencies lie; the political opposition, unstable by comparison, was rooted in the larger constituencies of the rural Indian population. Williams, who died in 1981, was a powerful, charismatic figure, who knew all too well the art of timing, when to speak and when to remain silent; and he faced only one serious challenge in his 25 years in power. That was in 1970, when an army mutiny and a black power movement – part of a regional upheaval that was felt during that period in several parts of the Caribbean – threatened for a while to depose him.

Williams made Trinidad and Tobago a republic in 1976 – a move which the far more radical government of Michael Manley in Jamaica never made – but the country remains a member of the Commonwealth with a moderate and respected international image. The head of state is a non-executive President; the elected government is headed by a Prime Minister, and there are two Houses of Parliament. The House of Representatives consists of elected members from 36 constituencies, while the non-elected Senate contains 31 members – 16 nominated by the government, six by the opposition, and nine (the 'independents') by the President. The system is essentially the British Westminster system, with Parliament and the judiciary balancing the power of the government. Free elections have been held regularly every five years since 1956, and by the mid 1980's the PNM had won every one of them, consistently controlling around two-thirds of the 36 seats.

The Economy

Like most of the Caribbean, Trinidad and Tobago developed as an agricultural nation, producing commodities for the developed world – mainly sugar, but also cocoa, coffee, citrus fruit – and importing manufactured goods in return. But, although sugar cane is still grown in central Trinidad, the industry has no real future; Trinidad and Tobago is one of the highest cost sugar producers in the world, but even low-cost producers are coming to terms with the fact that the days of growing cane sugar for export are over. It was one of Eric

Williams's accomplishments that he taught Trinidad and Tobago to think beyond export commodities to industrial production fuelled by natural gas.

Oil has long been the real backbone of the economy, a reliable revenue earner which made it possible not to bother too much about tourism or about building a manufacturing and industrial sector, at least with any great urgency. Trinidad and Tobago's own crude oil was refined partly at home and partly in the United States, extra crude was imported from Africa and the East for local refining, and the export of oil products in various forms provided the economy with its foundation. The oil price rises of the early 1970's not only snatched the economy back from the jaws of financial crisis, but produced – by Caribbean standards – very large financial surpluses.

Williams grasped the opportunity and established – at Point Lisas on Trinidad's west coast – a complex of heavy industrial plants all using offshore natural gas, which could generate new income when oil revenues declined, as they inevitably did. Thus Trinidad and Tobago swiftly developed a heavy industry sector alongside its somewhat stagnant agriculture, its small manufacturing and light industry, and its traditional importing businesses. In the early 1980's the oil boom ended at about the same time as the shock waves of international recession began to be felt in the region. Trinidad and Tobago is still the wealthiest of the English-speaking Caribbean states; but the resulting pressure on the economy, and particularly the need to end dependence on oil and diversify production, will show, in the remaining years of the century, how valid Williams's strategy was.

During the mid 1980's, the objective was to emerge from the boom years not merely intact but slimmer, more efficient. New emphasis was placed on the small manufacturing and tourism sectors, and on non-oil exports; Trinidad and Tobago began to seek new trading opportunities in the Far East as well as in traditional markets. Although foreign reserves fell rapidly between 1982 and 1985 (from nearly TT$8 billion to well below $3 billion), tough import and currency controls were introduced, the threatened balance of payments problem seemed to be coming under control and there was a growing trade surplus.

Even oil production was creeping up again after a steady decline from the 1978/79 peak of nearly 230,000 barrels a day; a second methanol plant was about to take shape in Point Fortin, and

TRINTOC, the national oil company, had taken control of the former Texaco refinery at Pointe a Pierre and was struggling to get the refining industry back on its feet. There were signs of a more positive collaboration between the government and the private sector: some of the red tape surrounding trade and investment procedures was being cut away, and leading businessmen were placed at the head of several government concerns including the Industrial Development Corporation and the Export Development Corporation. Although the adjustment process was putting severe pressure on businesses and jobs – unemployment had climbed to around 14 per cent – the outcome seemed likely to be a stronger and more efficient business sector.

Living

Neither political nor economic changes, however, make much difference to the lifestyle and character of Trinidad and Tobago, and the year proceeds very much as it has done for generations. Christmas is still a big event, requiring not only extensive spring cleaning and redecoration at home but a substantial list of seasonal excitements: parang music, black (fruit) cakes, sorrel and ginger beer, ham, enormous expenditure on gifts, imitation Christmas trees, extensive socialising, Bing Crosby on the radio. Old Year's night (December 31) is a night of obligatory partying, and the new year begins with a welcome public holiday. Between Christmas and Ash Wednesday comes the Carnival season: calypso, steelbands, masquerading, uninterrupted parties. The weeks of Lent are a quieter time, occupied in alternate years by the national Music Festival.

Those early weeks of the year, perhaps from mid-December, are the coolest: the dry season, when the sky is (usually) clear, the light is strong, the breeze is brisk, the colours are vivid and deep. It is the time of flying kites, of cricket, sailing, hiking. After Carnival, it begins to get hotter and more humid, and around the end of May the wet season usually begins, lasting on and off through the rest of the year. (The Caribbean hurricane belt, incidentally, lies to the north, rarely posing any threat to Trinidad and Tobago). The year moves on through a series of festivals and holidays and long weekends: Easter, Whitsun, Corpus Christi, Labour Day (June 19), Emancipation Day (August 1), Independence Day (August 31),

The Carnival season reaches a climax in two days of music and masquerade before the rigours of Ash Wednesday descend

11

Republic Day (September 24), the religious festivals of Divali and Eid-ul-Fitr; through the quiet summer holiday and back into the pre-Christmas season – the first carols usually invade the radio during October.

But of all these seasons – during which the physical seasons change only slightly – the key is Carnival. That is when Trinidad and Tobago is most itself, when its instinctive qualities of energy, tolerance, good humour and invention are most visible and most in harmony. Carnivals are essentially about masquerade, and Trinidad and Tobago's people are masters of the art of role-playing; but the Carnival role is natural, the real thing. As we shall see later, the Carnival is not only a celebration and a catharsis: it is also an industry of surprising energy and ingenuity, a creative process involving much of the population and fiercely resistant to undue control.

Transition

The image, of course, is that the Trinidad and Tobago lifestyle is easygoing and carefree, like the rest of the Caribbean, if not more so. Most myths have an element of truth, including this one; the Caribbean has so far imported only a few of the available metropolitan anxieties. Yet no culture is without its worries; even the straw-hatted minstrel has to pay for his guitar. And the swiftness of the modernisation process in Trinidad and Tobago, and the society's openness to North American lifestyles, have created tensions. The visitor may wonder at inefficiencies of bureaucracy and infrastructure, in the light of Trinidad and Tobago's comparative affluence; at traffic jams and corrugated roads (though do not forget the new highways); at the contrast between sophisticated ideas and ponderous bureaucratic obstacles. He may wonder at electrical 'outages' or workers who get up at 4.30 a.m. and hit the road by 5.00 in order to 'beat the traffic'.

It is partly that Trinidad and Tobago, like many other developing states (particularly oil producers), has had to cram decades of development into a few short years in its drive towards modernisation and high living standards. It is also that the national psyche insists on a very high degree of individual freedom. That produces a tolerant society, but also a society prone to inefficiencies. Rapid modernisation in a mixed and complex population has involved not only a delicate economic balance, but a delicate trade-off between freedom and efficiency, between tolerance and order. If Trinidad and Tobago seems sometimes to err on the side of individual freedom and tolerance, perhaps it feels that is the more congenial price to pay.

The period of transition which began in the 1970's and continued in the 1980's in the wake of the oil boom is likely to go on for some years yet. It has given Trinidad and Tobago both opportunities and tensions that most of its neighbours have barely felt. In Caribbean terms, the society has become affluent, familiar with high consumer prices and shopping trips to Miami; it has evolved sophisticated tastes and a people anxious to be accepted as a developed society. Its capital, Port of Spain, has been changing dramatically, with its old colonial buildings giving way to high-rise towers, its narrow streets clogged with new cars. Its traditional calypso has been changing too as singers try to streamline it for international marketing. Every year the Carnival itself is inflamed by controversies over control and finance, over how far the festival can be commercialised without losing its popular roots.

Yet in other ways Trinidad and Tobago changes hardly at all. Its basic flavour can be found easily enough in the time-worn images which make Trinidadians and Tobagonians in other countries intensely nostalgic for their own country. Examples? The panyards in the early days of the Carnival season, and the intentness with which the players absorb the year's tunes, note by note, phrase by phrase. The Queen's Park Savannah in the early evening, with its crowds of joggers, exercisers and strollers, Indian women selling oysters or roasting corn, coconut vendors picking nuts from their truck and slicing them open with a cutlass. The forested cliffs of the north coast on the way to Maracas Bay, fishermen pulling in their nets in Mayaro or Speyside, the white sand of Pigeon Point, Scarlet Ibis flying home to roost as the sun goes down on the Caroni Swamp.

Like many other countries, Trinidad and Tobago is anxious for enthusiasm in its visitors. It is accustomed to being praised for its warmth and hospitality and friendliness, for its steel orchestras and calypso, its spectacular Carnival. But it is an intensely proud and individualistic country too, accustomed to going its own way. The visitor who gets on best in Trinidad and Tobago will be outgoing without being patronising, sensitive to the pressures which agitate the society and the forces that hold it together; he will not be put off by defensiveness if he encounters it, nor see mere inefficiency in a necessary tolerance. He will sense a wish for respect and equality. The visitor who can do all that, and play mas' too, should find Trinidad and Tobago warming to him.

2

Evolution – Trinidad

Long before a restless Genoese sea captain known as Don Cristobal Colon set sail from Spain with a head full of dreams to make the first contact between the old world and the new – the first documented one, anyway – the Caribbean islands were well populated. Over the centuries, perhaps as early as 6,000 BC, Amerindian tribes had moved up the island chain from the South American coast. The two we know most about are the Arawaks, who were farmers, hunters and fishermen with a well-developed if simple system of tribal communities and chiefs, and the more belligerent Caribs who in both senses of the phrase came after them. Both groups probably

The statue of Christopher Columbus looks gravely down over the oldest part of Port of Spain

15

had settlements in the island which they probably knew as Iere when Columbus arrived.

It had been a tough voyage. Columbus had headed further south than on his first two voyages, again into unknown regions; supplies had run low, his ships had been becalmed for days, the crew had threatened mutiny. Columbus had begged successfully for three more days; and on the third, July 31, 1498, he sighted land and called it La Trinidad in honour of the Trinity – though legend insists that three hills on the horizon had something to do with it. What Columbus had seen was Trinidad's south-eastern tip; he sailed into the southern channel which now bears his name, paused briefly on the south coast (the encounter is still re-enacted in the village of Moruga, and Discovery Day was a national holiday till 1984), swept in the strong currents around the island's south-western peninsula and anchored.

The island pleased him. Exaggerating somewhat, he reported to King Ferdinand and Queen Isabella of Spain that he saw not only houses and people but 'very fair lands, lands as beautiful and green as the gardens of Valencia in the month of March'.

He also saw a large canoe manned by Arawak Indians in short tunics, armed with bows and arrows and shields. They found Columbus just as curious as he found them. The first contact was not too auspicious. Hoping to encourage the Arawaks on board, Columbus ordered some of his crew to perform a Spanish dance with drum accompaniment, which the Arawaks understandably took as an act of war, letting off a volley of arrows. The Spaniards replied with crossbows.

Columbus sailed on, exploring the Gulf and finally braving the fierce currents off north-west Trinidad to sail back into the open Atlantic on August 14; the narrow northern passage he called the Dragon's Mouth, the southern one the Serpent's Mouth. It is unlikely that he saw the silhouette of Tobago on the far horizon before striking out further west along the South American coast, the Spanish Main, though many historians claim that he did.

Spain

For several decades, Iere's Amerindians watched these strangely-clothed, strangely-coloured visitors in their big ships. At first it was a matter of Spanish raids in search of forced labour for projects elsewhere, like diving for pearls off the island of Margarita. The first two Spanish missionaries to venture into Trinidad paid the price for these press-gang tactics: they were executed. The first serious attempt to establish Spanish authority was made by Don Antonio Sedeno, a restless official with a somewhat chequered past who had himself transferred out of the colonial service in Puerto Rico to become Captain General of the virtually unknown island of Trinidad in 1530. But in spite of a series of bloody skirmishes with the Amerindians, both in the south and around Cu-Mucurapo (now a suburb of Port of Spain), he made little impact. Trinidad, nominally Spanish, remained the most neglected and least known corner of the Spanish empire, an island with no known resources, at best a staging post for dreamers on their way to El Dorado, the fabulous city which was supposed to lie not too far away in the South American interior.

One such dreamer, Don Antonio de Berrio y Oruna, established the first real Spanish foothold in Trinidad at the end of the 1500's, more than a century after Columbus passed by. He had his lieutenant, Domingo de Vera, found a small town some way inland by the Caroni River, and later made it his own base. This was the tiny settlement of San José de Oruna – now the Port of Spain suburb of St Joseph – where, in 1592, de Vera ritually marked out the sites of the governor's house, the *cabildo* (council), the church and the prison. In the early days, San José's population was about 20 plus a few soldiers; de Berrio managed to keep the Amerindians at bay but never to control them. British explorers were prowling the area already: Robert Dudley showed up in 1595, closely followed by Sir Walter Raleigh, who was out of favour with Queen Elizabeth I and anxious to find El Dorado himself. He studied the coast carefully, caulked his ships at the Pitch Lake ('most excellent goode, and melteth not in the sun as Pitch of Norway'), then settled an old score with de Berrio by kidnapping him and burning down San José.

For two centuries more Trinidad was to remain a forgotten colonial backwater. The Spanish settlers tried to sell tobacco to the occasional passing ship; there was the occasional skirmish or attempt at foreign settlement; the Dutch may have brought in the first 400 African slaves. But in 1640 the Spanish governor was complaining that he did not even have a pair of decent shoes; in

17

1662 his successor moaned that nobody had seen a Spanish ship in 30 years. Capuchin Fathers were despatched in 1687 to establish missions in Trinidad and thus assert Spanish authority through evangelization; but the good fathers so exasperated the Amerindians that several were murdered at San Francisco de las Arenales in 1699, an incident that led to furious Spanish recriminations and a further depletion of the Amerindian community.

Part of the reason for Spain's neglect of Trinidad was that the former was already becoming a second-rate naval power and had over-reached its imperial resources. By the turn of the century, Spain's navy was only a quarter of the size of Britain's or Holland's, and most of its ships were busy on the treasure routes far to the west of Trinidad. Trinidad's governor reported to the Viceroy of New Granada at Bogota, more than two months' journey away. So the Spanish settlers were left to themselves, scratching a living from the plantations which they hacked out of the forests and worked with Amerindian labour. After tobacco they turned to cocoa, which for a while became important to Trinidad – important enough to bring the infamous Blackbeard scurrying into the Gulf in 1716 in pursuit of a cocoa ship – but in time that too collapsed. By 1733 there were only 162 adult males that the authorities could find to count, 28 of whom could be classified as pure Spanish – and that was before the 1739 smallpox epidemic. San José remained in such a miserable state, its *cabildo* so hopelessly impotent, that in 1757, an incoming governor took one look at it and retired to the coastal village of Puerto de l'Espana, which was to become the new capital.

By this time, all Trinidad's neighbours had been developed as prosperous slave colonies by their British, French or Dutch masters. Spain began to grasp that unless it did something with Trinidad, one of the other European powers would. Thus, from about 1776, Spain began trying to attract foreign settlers into Trinidad. One early powerful advocate of this policy was Roumé de St Laurent, a French settler in Grenada with a keen eye for development prospects, who reinforced Spain's growing conviction that Trinidad had real potential if only it could acquire a population. In 1783 Spain promised land in Trinidad to anybody willing to go there so long as they were nationals of a country allied with Spain and were Roman Catholics. In practice, that meant Frenchmen and definitely not the British. An additional promise of more land encouraged settlers to bring with them as many slaves as possible.

18

Sugar cane: the reality behind slavery and indenture, and for more than a century the backbone of the economy

The response was good; the prospect of new, fertile land in Trinidad excited many French settlers struggling along on older lands in Grenada, St Lucia, Martinique and Guadeloupe. Trinidad began to experience a boom. In 1784 Spain sent out by far the ablest of its governors, Don José Maria Chacon, a well-educated man, comparatively liberal and reform-minded, fluent in French – which was an asset, since the French already outnumbered Spaniards on the *cabildo* by over three to one. Chacon transformed Port of Spain, enlarging and improving it, building fortifications on the surrounding hills. He introduced a more liberal slave code, developed San Fernando – Trinidad's second town – and kept the peace between the old disgruntled Spanish settlers and the brash new Frenchmen, whose numbers were swelled in the 1790's by an influx of Republicans for whom Chacon had little taste. Under Chacon, Trinidad's population tripled to almost 18,000; of that figure, barely 1,000 were Amerindians, just over 2,000 were white, and over 10,000 – well over half the total – were African slaves. The rest were 'free coloureds', a property-owning coloured class, something unknown in the other islands. But Spain's new policy had come too

19

late. In the wake of the French Revolution, France and England were at war, and already their navies had been skirmishing around Trinidad. In 1796 Spain declared war on England and, as Chacon feared, one early result was that the large English fleet in the Caribbean, which had been busy putting down French-inspired revolts in the British colonies, turned its attention to Trinidad, this juicy, suddenly booming Spanish outpost. Under Sir Ralph Abercromby, the English arrived off Chaguaramas, near Port of Spain, early in 1797, far outnumbering the Spanish force of five ships. The Spanish admiral, Don Sebastien Ruiz de Apodaca, preferring discretion to valour, set fire to his ships to avoid their capture, and scrambled ashore. The English marched into Port of Spain and forced Chacon to surrender; today, he and Abercromby are commemorated in two parallel streets in downtown Port of Spain.

England

The English thus found themselves in charge of a prosperous French colony under Spanish law, complete with 150 new sugar estates laid out during the boom of the previous 15 years. Slightly bemused, they retained Spanish law and existing office-holders; but, to exercise the real control, Abercromby appointed one of his own officers, Thomas Picton, as the first British governor, and moved on, leaving Picton to keep Trinidad British and secure for the duration of the war with Spain.

Picton was very much the simple soldier faced with security problems: there was the danger of Spanish counter-attack and of trouble from the French or the slaves or both, not to mention shock waves from the French Revolution, the slave uprising in Haiti and the Spanish-American war of independence.

Picton quickly showed a taste for strong government. Becoming a slave owner himself, he saw the slave and 'free coloured' classes as the prime security threat and instituted ruthless policies to keep both in check. Unconstrained by British overlords, he used his full authority, employing torture, whippings and burnings, mutilations and executions; a gallows was set up in front of Government House and was used with enthusiasm.

But when peace was made with Spain in 1801–2, Trinidad was not returned to its former owners: it was confirmed as a British colony. Picton's excesses became a political embarrassment, and he was removed. But Britain was left with the problem of what to do with Trinidad. To develop the island as a sugar-and-slave colony like its neighbours would require at least 250,000 slaves, 12 times the number available in 1808. It was too late for that; feeling against slavery was building up in the British Parliament, and there were serious doubts about how much longer Caribbean slave societies would be economically attractive. Britain did not want to set up an elected assembly, because the structure of Trinidad's population would ensure that it was controlled by non-British interests: the 'free coloured' class outnumbered whites by more than two to one, and less than half the white community was British. Britain's solution was to make Trinidad a Crown Colony, controlled directly from London through a Governor, and a model slave colony in which the situation of slaves would be steadily improved. If it worked, the Trinidad model would then be applied in the older Caribben slave colonies.

But it did not work. Picton and his successors wanted a fullblown slave colony like Barbados or Jamaica. The slave owners thwarted all British attempts to strengthen slave rights and control the worst abuses, a policy which became steadily more desirable as the anti-slavery lobby grew stronger in England, and thus hastened their own demise.

But even though it failed, London's 'amelioration' policy profoundly affected the shape of Trinidad's future society. Slaves poured into Trinidad during the last years of Spanish rule and the first four or five under the British, but then the influx slowed down; slave trading was abolished in 1807, though an illegal trade into Trinidad continued for years, with slaves passed off as domestic servants. But the net result was that slavery in Trinidad was very different from the experience of the other Caribbean colonies. It was on a smaller scale, it did not last as long, and the black-white divisions were complicated by the 'free coloured' class among whom there were many slave owners.

Trinidad saw no major slave uprisings. But the slave community evolved a sort of underground network of linked groups which maintained a secret world of their own which was quite separate from the plantation world: a world of kings and queens, courts and powerful medicine men (here lies the root of today's Trinidad Carnival). Some of this came out into the open in 1805 when

Fort George above Port of Spain: the major British defence after Trinidad was seized from Spain

Governor Hislop announced that he had uncovered a Christmas Day plot against some slave owners and crushed it with customary brutality.

The first decades of the 1800's must have been traumatic for the French settlers who had hurried into Trinidad at the end of the Spanish period, filled with enthusiasm for a new frontier. The British gradually tightened their hold on the island's Catholic society, imposing English language and laws, trying to replace Catholicism with the alien rituals of the Church of England. The 'free coloureds' fought hard for their rights, ultimately with success; slavery, which had seemed so vital for development, withered and died; even the old *cabildo*, long faded into impotence but still a rallying point for the older settlers and a useful obstacle to British meddling, was abolished in 1840 and replaced with a British-style town council. And in the wake of the British decision to abolish slavery altogether, Trinidad was haunted by a crucial uncertainty: how was it going to survive, let alone develop, as a sugar and cocoa producer of any significance? Who exactly was going to do the work?

India

That question baffled London for years. Various hare-brained schemes were floated: indentured labourers from Ireland and Scotland, army and navy men, European immigrants, labour from other Caribbean islands, even Amerindians. China was tried, but most of the workers who came quickly went home again. The former slaves showed no inclination for returning to the estates on any terms and drifted into their own smallholdings, into the towns and villages, into cocoa. The British tried Portuguese workers, ex-slaves from other islands and from America, freed slaves from Sierra Leone and St Helena, European emigrants, Madeirans. Many wilted, many more went home; the problem remained unsolved.

In the end India rescued Trinidad's planters and fundamentally changed the island's population structure. India had already supplied labour to Ceylon, Mauritius and British Guiana; between 1845 and 1917, almost 144,000 Indians arrived in Trinidad as indentured labourers from halfway across the globe, entitled to a return journey after five or ten years but facing tough, near-slave conditions in the meantime. They came mainly from Uttar Pradesh, Bihar and Oudh, some from Bengal and Punjab, through the ports of Calcutta and Madras, in search of a miraculous escape from economic stagnation and a new life in the Caribbean. The majority were Hindus, with a substantial minority of Moslems. Because of this inflow, sugar remained king in Trinidad till the end of the century.

Many of the Indian workers did not return to India. They bought land in Trinidad, or traded their return tickets for 10-acre lots. They settled mainly in the sugar lands of central and south Trinidad, and went into small shopkeeping and trading, or into cocoa or rice. By 1871 a quarter of the population was Indian. Because families could stick together, institutions and social structures survived the transition; but because the host society offered little status or trust, the Indians remained well down on the social ladder, protecting themselves through traditions of caste and religion, family and community. There were strong missionary efforts to Christianise and Westernise the Indian community, but they met with only partial success. There was little intermarrying – even today, the Romeo and Juliet theme (African boy, Indian girl, or vice versa) surfaces on the local stage – and Indian participation in politics was slow to come.

Hierarchy

So, while its neighbours retained their black-and-white simplicities, Trinidad's society became complex and hierarchical. At the top was a strong white élite of dubious cohesion – a tightknit Catholic (mainly French) group, aristocratic and property owning and keeping its bloodline pure, coexisting uneasily with the upstarts, the later English colonists. The two tussled over explosive cultural questions like religion, law and language until Governor Gordon managed to defuse much of the tension in the 1860's.

Below the white élite was a fast-growing middle class of black and mixed race people, successors of the 'free coloureds' of pre-abolition days: teachers, lawyers, doctors, clerks. The education system that developed from the 1850's made upward mobility possible, and Port of Spain got its first black mayor from this class as early as 1867. Its political influence grew steadily, and it produced many of the voices which articulated demands for reform.

At the bottom of the ladder sat the majority: creole ex-slaves (mainly Catholic and patois-speaking), immigrants from other islands (mainly Protestant and English-speaking), former American slaves, Spanish-speaking 'peons' from Venezuela, and the survivors of the many experiments in imported labour. Here the rule was poverty, exclusion from political life and little hope of education or social status. There was a steady drift into Port of Spain where families crowded into barrack-yards with little hope of jobs; but the majority was still rural, working on smallholdings or in cocoa. Frustrations erupted in Carnival clashes. Some African communities managed to hold on to their traditions, like the Radas from Dahomey who settled in Belmont; but you could be jailed or flogged for practising virtually any African ritual. This was the period when African traditions were grafted on to newer Christian faiths, when calypso was preparing to emerge in its modern form, and when – with drumming banned by the British – people began to search for substitutes, a search which culminated in the steel bands of the next century.

And gradually the demand for political change made itself heard. The British had set up a Council of Government in 1831, consisting of officials and citizens nominated by the Governor, but then made no further concessions to democracy for nearly a century. Middle class dissent fed on demands for elected members on the

Council, and by the end of the century had begun to produce organised opposition. The Trinidad Workingmen's Association emerged in 1897, the Ratepayers' Association and branches of the Pan African Association in 1901, all preparing for the trade unions and political parties of the future. The Ratepayers' Association and its angry protest about water – the peg, really, for much broader and deeper grievances – led to a bloody clash with police in 1903 during which Port of Spain's administrative headquarters, the grandiloquent Red House, was burned down.

3

Evolution – Tobago

Whether the wandering Columbus actually spotted Tobago in 1498 is not certain. He gave the name Bellaforma to an island on the horizon which might have been Tobago, but did not land there. Tobago remained isolated, without the privilege of being 'discovered', for many decades more, its mainly Carib inhabitants undisturbed.

Most historians give up the task of trying to disentangle what happened in Tobago in the two-and-a-half centuries or so after Columbus disappeared over the horizon. It was not that Tobago was short of activity: it was simply that the island did not belong clearly to anyone, and instead became the plaything of Dutch, French and English raiders, pirates and buccaneers, settlers from Latvia and intruders from Trinidad. These followed so quickly on one another's heels that many 'captures' were really a few days spent laying waste to somebody else's settlement. Whether Tobago changed hands 24 times or 31 times during those turbulent years depends on what you count as 'changing hands'.

Eighty-two years after Columbus, English seamen passing by reported that Tobago was uninhabited, which was almost certainly not true. England began claiming the island from a distance as early as 1608. In 1625 a party from Barbados, accompanied by their chaplain, the Reverend Nicholas Leverton, B.A. (Oxon.), attempted to land, but was fiercely attacked by the Caribs, and the survivors – including Mr Leverton, who was wounded in the head – only escaped by swimming ignominiously back to their ship. By 1629, the Dutch had probably established a settlement called New Walcheren, but could not withstand the dual pressures of disease and Carib aggression. There may also have been an English settlement around the same time.

Courland Bay: some of the earliest settlers in Tobago came from Latvia and made a home here

Then came the Spanish; perpetually nervous about hostile forces in Tobago, they launched an attack from Trinidad and found a small colony of international vagrants sheltering among rudimentary fortifications. After them came an unexpected force: hopeful settlers sent out by the Duke of Courland, to whom Tobago had been granted by the King of England. Courland, on the Baltic Sea, later became part of Latvia, which is now part of the Soviet Union, though so far Moscow has neglected to pursue the old Duke's claim.

The Courlanders made several attempts from 1639 to establish and hold permanent settlements, skirmishing with the Caribs and the English and being rudely repelled by the Dutch. The dispute went on for decades. As late as 1731, with the encouragement of the King of Poland, the Duke was still trying to get Tobago back, and even generously offered it to the King of Sweden, who tried to establish his own colony there, rather late in the day, in 1733.

In the meantime, the English, Dutch and French were periodically wrecking each other's settlements and fortifications, while pirates cheerfully made Tobago their base in the lull between conflicts. On one occasion the French, with 25 volunteers and two

27

loud drums, tricked the English into surrendering the island by pretending that a huge French military force was poised for attack. By 1749, England and France were weary and agreed that Tobago should be neutral, an arrangement which pleased the pirates and naturally did not last.

England and France

The first power to keep a foothold on Tobago for any length of time was England, which 'captured' the island again in 1762 and began establishing longer-term settlements and planting sugar, cotton and indigo. The English gave the little capital an unmistakably English name – Scarborough – and set up an Assembly which held its first session in 1768. They tried to make Tobago part of a federation with Grenada, St Vincent and Dominica. By 1771, the population was 5,084, all but 368 of whom were slaves. There were sporadic slave revolts and after the sugar crop was wrecked by ants in 1775 the settlers turned to cotton. The population built up to 13,000, still 80 per cent slaves. In 1778 Tobago even had to fend off an American squadron; the estates mounted guns.

Then, in 1781, just around the time that the first French settlers were trickling into Trinidad, the French snatched Tobago from the English and held it for twelve years, giving the island its first attempt at serious economic development. The French tried to establish a free port (without success – the idea is still on Tobago's agenda), raised local taxes, and introduced incentives to develop sugar, coffee, cocoa, cotton and indigo plantations. They tried to bribe French settlers in Trinidad to come across to Tobago, offered tax concessions to boost the population, and tried to seduce settlers away from other islands too. Under the French, Tobago began to look more like a conventional Caribbean sugar-and-slave colony. The population grew to 15,000, of whom 94 per cent were slaves; and at one time the island supported 37 sugar factories and 99 cotton factories.

But the British recaptured Tobago in 1793 and set about wiping out French influence there. They were to remain in control, almost uninterrupted, until independence in 1962. For a year or so in 1802–3, Tobago had to be formally returned to France under the Treaty of Amiens (following which Tobago's Legislative Council, with admirable pragmatism, enthusiastically endorsed the decision of Napoleon Bonaparte − who was about to plunge the western world into another twelve years of war − to appoint himself First Consul for life). But the English regarded this as a mere irritation: the following year they landed on the island and once more kicked the French out.

During the 19th century, Tobago was ahead of Trinidad in at least one way, however: it was a self-governing colony with an elected assembly (even if the electorate was a mere 102). For a while, sugar prospered; but it depended, of course, on slavery, and abolition in 1834 forced the island's already inefficient plantations into crisis. Like Trinidad, Tobago embarked on a desperate search for alternative labour: England, Europe, other Caribbean islands, ex-slaves from Africa and America. But, unlike Trinidad, it never found a labour source big enough to keep it going. In the 1840's, Britain equalized the duties on West Indian and foreign sugar, ending the Caribbean monopoly; in Tobago this triggered a move away from sugar into cocoa and coconuts, and a stream of migration into Trinidad. Protesting loudly, the estates developed a system called *metairie*, under which planters divided the produce of their estates on a co-operative basis with their labourers: it was a sign of how desperate they were getting.

Union with Trinidad

Tobago's crisis came to a head in the last three decades of the 19th century. In 1874 England set up a single-chamber Assembly with an elected majority; but within two years, after riots in Roxborough, Tobago lost its Assembly and its embryo democracy altogether and was brought under direct rule from London as a Crown Colony. A British commission appeared and found Tobago virtually bankrupt; it recommended a federation with St Vincent, St Lucia, Grenada and possibly Dominica (fifty years earlier, a similar proposal, for federating Tobago with Grenada and St Vincent under Barbados, had come to nothing).

Then in 1884 the London company which represented over half Tobago's sugar estates collapsed. Land values crashed, production and revenue plunged and it became clear that Tobago could not support itself any longer. The problem hung like a millstone around

Fort King George, built by the British in the 1770s, commands the approach to Scarborough and Rockly Bay

the neck of the Colonial Office which, as usual, had no clear solution. Thus to save costs and inconvenience, and to be rid of the problem as quickly as possible, London decided on a course which found little favour in either Tobago or Trinidad: to link the two islands in one state. In January 1889 they were united under one governor, with a common judiciary and code of laws; Tobago retained local financial control. In October 1898 the process was completed: Tobago became a Ward of the new colony of Trinidad and Tobago, and the islands merged their finances too.

4

Evolution – Trinidad and Tobago

The statue of Captain Arthur Cipriani surveys the traffic on Independence Square

In the 20th century, the road led inevitably towards independence and the challenges beyond. The new colony experienced a cycle of hard times, industrial unrest and concessions from the British, a process which threw up a succession of charismatic political leaders, and which was punctuated by short-lived periods of boom.

The First World War produced the first major wave of industrial and social change. Marcus Garvey's adventures in the United States were in the air. Men who volunteered for war service and were given a taste of European racism for their trouble, came home with their political consciousness sharpened. One of them was Captain Arthur Cipriani, who came from a white creole family of Corsican descent, and who, in 1923, became President of the rejuvenated Trinidad Workingmen's Association (TWA). He was popular, a powerful orator, charismatic and committed to change; when Britain introduced a limited franchise in 1925 and called the first national elections, in which only six per cent of the population could vote, Cipriani stood for the TWA in Port of Spain, won the seat and for the next few years dominated the young labour movement. In the Legislative Council he functioned as a one-man opposition, pushing for constitutional reform and industrial improvement; he began to draw support from the Indian community too, helped by Adrian Cola Rienzi (whose real name was Krishna Deonarine), who became president of the TWA's San Fernando branch in 1925.

The 1930's were a tough time for Trinidad and Tobago, as they were for many other countries; the recession and the dwindling prosperity of the traditional industries produced demonstrations and hunger marches in 1933–4. An oil strike in 1935 threw up a new popular leader in the south – Tubal Uriah Butler, a Grenadian who had come to work in the oilfields after the war, an immensely charismatic figure with the aura of an Old Testament prophet. As Cipriani's influence faded, and with it that of the Trinidad Labour Party which succeeded the TWA, Butler and Rienzi formed the Trinidad Citizens' League, one of several new labour organisations that evolved during the decade. It was a time of cultural upheaval too, with a lively literary movement dominated by men like C. L. R. James, Albert Gomes, Alfred Mendes and Ralph de Boissiere.

The big flare-up came in 1937. In June, a critical oilfield strike began, which escalated rapidly as the authorities clumsily tried to arrest Butler, who went into hiding. Two policemen and 12

32

civilians were killed. Governor Fletcher favoured a policy of conciliation – Britain after all was anxious to keep Trinidad and Tobago stable at a time of growing world crisis – but pressure from the oil companies and the white élite forced a harder line, and Butler was put on trial for sedition. Rienzi was able to organise both oil and sugar workers and by 1939 was heading a Trade Union Congress representing a broad range of labour interests.

The Second World War did much to get the economy moving again, particularly as the United States established an air base and a naval base in Trinidad as part of a land-lease deal with Britain. Trinidad was the wartime assembly point for tankers carrying Caribbean oil across the Atlantic to North Africa and Europe: the Caribbean became infested with German submarines trying to stop this traffic (which incidentally forced the islands into setting up an airline, now the Trinidad and Tobago national carrier BWIA). The Americans built several of Trinidad's major roads, including the north coast road to Maracas Bay, and invented rum and coke; they exuded an aura of affluence and machismo and treated workers – sometimes – as equals, a novel experience. Their influence, in other words, was profound.

During the war, trade union activity, like the Carnival, was restricted, and Butler was detained; in the post-war transition period it became clear that Butler's day was done and he was defeated in the 1946 elections by Albert Gomes, a heavyweight of Portuguese descent, who was to dominate the political scene until the mid 1950's. That first post-war decade was a time of agitation for full representative government and the search for a stable party system – the Legislative Council still had a majority of nominated members. In 1946 and 1950, the labour-based parties were still too fragmented to give birth to the nationalist party which Trinidad and Tobago needed to move it towards self-government and independence. Although Butler's party won the largest single block of seats in 1950, the British managed to manoeuvre him away from power, and the 1950–56 government was dominated by Gomes.

Oil and Sugar

The economic backbone of Trinidad and Tobago was already oil. The industry was one of the oldest in the world, dating back to

The larger of the two refineries, at Pointe a Pierre, which was acquired by the state company TRINTOC from Texaco in 1985

1857, though early activity fizzled out for lack of capital. But when it revived in the early years of the 20th century, there was a herculean programme of clearing forest and hauling equipment by hand into the remote drilling sites in south Trinidad. By 1946 Trinidad was supplying 65 per cent of the British Empire's oil production – which explains why the British were willing to make concessions in the name of stability and industrial peace.

The refining industry grew up during the war, and by 1943 oil accounted for 80 per cent of all Trinidad and Tobago's exports (virtually the same level as in 1984); the country was well on the way to becoming a classic oil economy, heavily dependent for its prosperity on one capital-intensive industry. Not that sugar disappeared: production reached 134,000 tons in 1937 despite the recession, though little of the proceeds reached the sugar workers; and sugar was grown in Tobago until the 1930's too. After the war, sugar recovered and prospered in the 1940's and 1950's, reaching an average of 217,000 tons in 1958–63.

The only other major crop was cocoa, which enjoyed its golden years from 1870 to 1920 before falling into the doldrums. Manufacturing and hotel development began to evolve in the 1950's, and in Tobago tourism replaced agriculture as the economic lifeline. Tobago had otherwise done little better as a Ward than it had done as a self-governing colony; it was 1952 before electricity reached Scarborough and what progress Tobago did make was largely due to its relentless representative, A. P. T. James, who pushed the island's interest in the Legislative Council until 1961.

Towards Independence

But the decisive development was the emergence in early 1956 of the People's National Movement (PNM), a cohesive nationalist

Trinidad cocoa, long prized for its quality: the golden years were from 1870 to 1920

movement which eclipsed the squabbling labour-based parties and all the old-guard leaders. Unusually for the Caribbean, the PNM began as a middle-class party, the child of Dr Eric Williams, a formidable intellectual with equally formidable political skills. Williams had distinguished himself as a historian and university teacher in Britain and the United States; he returned to Trinidad in 1948 as deputy chairman of the Caribbean Research Council of the Caribbean Commission and soon became a powerful figure in public life. His books broke new ground and his public lectures, especially on Caribbean history (a subject which Williams had mastered, and of which he took a thorough-going anti-colonial view), won him a powerful following and awakened a sense of black nationalist pride.

In 1954–5, Williams's political influence grew strong enough for him to lay the foundations of a new nationalist party. That year he was fired by the Caribbean Commission, and his response was typically defiant: 'I was born here, and here I stay, with the people of Trinidad and Tobago . . . I am going to let down my bucket where I am, now, right here with you in the British West Indies.' He made the big square in central Port of Spain his rallying point: 'The only university at which I shall lecture in future is the University of Woodford Square, and its several branches throughout the length and breadth of Trinidad and Tobago.' The new party was lauched in January 1956 and swept into power later that year; Williams became Chief Minister. The PNM declared it was not leftist or socialist, but sought to unite capital and labour under a nationalist banner; it was highly selective about its members, and demanded total loyalty to its leadership.

Williams and the PNM steered Trinidad and Tobago to independence in 1962. The only political threat came from the tough Indian leader, Bhadase Maraj, who led a strong Democratic Labour Party (DLP) – embracing many of the remnants of the old parties – against the PNM in 1958 when elections were held in the new West Indies Federation, and won six of the ten seats available. Then, and in 1961, it seemed as if a dangerous pattern of ethnic voting was developing, with both sides appealing to racial solidarity – black creoles behind the PNM, Indians behind the DLP. In 1958–60 the PNM wore a more radical mask as it fought for the return of the Chaguaramas naval base from the Americans; the battle was won and the radicalism was quietly tempered. By 1962, the PNM's dominance was secure: the DLP had split, constitutional goals had been achieved, political boundaries had been drawn and the voting pattern was established that was to prove the most durable in the Caribbean – about a third of the seats going to successive opposition parties and centred in the sugar belt of south and central Trinidad, and the remaining two thirds – centred in the heavily Afro-Trinidadian, urban centres of north Trinidad – being held by the PNM.

In 1981 the PNM began its sixth consecutive five-year term. In 25 years it had faced few serious threats: the major one came in 1970, when 'black power' pressure combined with an army mutiny threatened Williams's government. But Williams rode the crisis. In 1973, with the economy near bankruptcy, he resigned; but almost immediately came the boom in oil prices which turned Trinidad and Tobago into the Caribbean's most affluent state during the 1970's, and Williams returned.

In 1971, the opposition boycotted elections and left the PNM in full control. In 1976, the newly-formed United Labour Front, born out of the previous year's upheaval in the sugar and oil belts, became the principal opposition party and the PNM lost Tobago to the Democratic Action Congress (DAC). Still complaining of neglect, Tobago had its House of Assembly restored in 1980, though with very limited powers; the DAC took control of it, and increased its majority there in 1984. Williams died in 1981 and was succeeded by George Chambers, one of the three PNM deputy leaders and a former finance minister. Later that year the party won its biggest election victory ever, even snatching a traditional opposition seat and preventing a newly formed opposition party – the Organisation for National Reconstruction, led by a former PNM Attorney General – from winning a single seat.

But the PNM soon seemed to be heading for a difficult period, marked by the end of the oil boom and the challenge of economic readjustment, as well as defeats in local government elections, the quiet erosion of traditional voting patterns and the prospect of an opposition united for the first time.

5

The Carnival

Well, history helps. But the way to understand today's Trinidad and Tobago, to see the country with its soul bared, is to join (or at least watch) the annual Carnival, which reaches its climax on the two days before Ash Wednesday.

Trinidad and Tobago without Carnival would be like Washington without intrigue or Salzburg without music. With its two offshoots, calypso and steel orchestras, it is an ear-splitting, insomniac orgy of movement and colour, a communal catharsis. It is what Trinidad and Tobago best likes to be known by, and what best defines the country's free spirit: to say it is the greatest show on earth will endear you for ever. And although it is far from being the only big or famous Carnival in the world, it is perhaps the most down-to-earth, the most participatory Carnival, the one that has stayed closest to the people and furthest from commercialism and empty show.

But taking the Carnival seriously is a full-time job. The season begins more or less at breakfast on Boxing Day and by the time the Old Year's parties come round all the talk is of whose new calypso is hot and sweet and who is joining which masquerade band. The serious devotee will get into training as the season advances with regular attendance at vast all-night *fetes* (parties), *jumping-up* (dancing) to three or four different bands. He will monitor the singers at half a dozen calypso *tents*, mostly drab union halls where teams of calypsonians deliver their satires, complaints, libels and dance tunes in a bid to win the year's Calypso Monarch title. He will keep tabs on dozens of steel orchestras practising nightly in empty city lots and struggling through several rounds of competition as Carnival and the Panorama competition approach.

Above all, he will sign up for a costume in one of the big

masquerade bands, disguise himself as a king, Roman centurion, butterfly, frog, warrior, tree, fish, emperor or whatever, and join thousands of revellers, Cabinet ministers, dock workers, lawyers, unemployed labourers, permanent secretaries and a surfeit of danc- ing women more given to revelation than disguise, in bands that dance through the streets for two days from one competition site to another until the sun goes down and the rum runs out.

Taking Carnival more seriously still means penetrating a vast network of cottage industries, ranging from costume construction and boot-making to steel-tempering and music arranging, which hold the Carnival together in an astonishing display of skilled and ingenious craft. It all drives moralistically-minded Trinidadians crazy, and many take refuge at the beach: Carnival, they moan, addles the nation's brains for the rest of the year, and if only Carnival productivity could be applied to conventional work . . .

How to Join In

Unlike Rio's, Trinidad and Tobago's Carnival, centred in Port of Spain but with smaller celebrations all over the two islands, is still largely spontaneous, locally-oriented and peaceful. There is much less chance of running into trouble in a Carnival crowd than on the New York subway: British police pay regular visits, trying to figure out how such large excited crowds manage to stay so amiable.

Fetes

The long sequence of pre-Carnival fetes, becoming steadily more enormous and euphoric as the season goes on, is really the training period, the leisurely warming-up, for the two Olympic days of Carnival.

Small, spontaneous fetes (the word is pronounced the French way, not the 'fate' that the English make of it) are liable to erupt anywhere at any time, at the click of a stereo switch or the uncapping of a rum bottle. There are house parties to which it is not too difficult to be invited. But the bigger, public events are organised and advertised in the press and charge admission fees. Several venues hold big traditional functions which hold the spotlight on a particular day: among them are the Yacht Club, the Oval (home of the Queen's Park Cricket Club), the St Augustine Tennis Club, and the Blood Bank (one of several all-day fetes). At some of these functions, Old Mas' bands (see below) parade and compete. Towards the end of the season every possible venue holds its own function, especially on the Saturday and Sunday night before Carnival.

The scene is basically the party scene from anywhere in the world, but enormously large and very energetic, spread over whole compounds, sports grounds and car parks with the largesse of a Hollywood set. Three or four bands are often at work, playing in different areas and including both brass and steel groups.

The visitor's best course is to shed as many inhibitions as possible early in the game. There is little chance of learning to move in the way that is instinctive to Trinidadians unless you are an accomplished mimic – for the dance movements are very distinctive and well defined, despite the appearance of spontaneity, and Trinidadians derive much amusement from the antics of Carnival guests more accustomed to the casual twitchings of metropolitan discotheques. The Carnival style is called *jumping up*; a fete is a *jump-up*. At its wildest, it's exactly that – both feet off the ground, hands high above the head, as the music screams a calypso climax. But there are gentler forms. One is called *chipping*, which is simply a shuffle, similar to the steps of a drunken man (so that it may come naturally after a while) and well suited to the long distances of the street masquerade. A slightly more energetic version has the arms oustretched (the precise angle is important but don't worry about that). *Wining* demands well-lubricated hips and something of the belly-dancer's skill, and is a reminder that Carnival dance has to do with body movement rather than steps.

But a Trinidad and Tobago fete is a good-natured, genuinely casual affair where it's easier to be over-dressed than under-dressed, and where nobody is going to look down a snobbish nose if you don't wine right; they probably won't notice anyway. Be prepared for thick crowds and to push your way to the bar, where you may have to pay a good price for a minimum quarter-bottle.

Tents

The calypso tents are open by the early days of the new year. Once they really were tents, places where the masquerade bands rehearsed their music; now they tend to occupy bare union meeting halls in spartan conditions. Perhaps 150 to 200 singers, only a handful of them full-time professionals, each with one or more new songs, spread out among the year's tents, forming teams of a couple of dozen. Each tent will have a handful of star singers led by a big name like Sparrow, Kitchener or Shadow; the supporting singers range from beginners to old-timers who never made it to the top of the ladder or who have since slipped off.

The repertoire often changes during the season and the standard improves too. There is a live resident band and the songs range from traditional styles (heavy on lyrics, with sharp political and social criticism) to modern party numbers where all the emphasis is on a fast, stylish beat. Only a few songs from each year's crop live on as 'classics'. The show is held together by an MC, usually a singer himself, with a good line in repartee and *picong* (good-humoured insult) and a large stock of risky jokes.

The better-known singers produce annual albums of their songs and enter the race for the Calypso Monarch's title. Roving judges select 24 singers from the various tents who then perform before a traditionally rowdy audience in San Fernando a week before Carnival. There, seven singers are chosen to challenge the reigning Monarch at the Dimanche Gras show on the Sunday night before Carnival. There is a second calypso contest too, which depends less on formal judging and more on popular acclaim. As the masquerade bands move across the main competition site on Carnival days, the accompanying bands play one of the year's calypsos; whichever song is most played becomes the year's Road March and its singer the Road March King.

Panyards

The steel orchestras practise nightly from early in the season, well into the small hours, and are quite used to casual listeners dropping by. Their home bases are empty city lots or wherever enough space can be found to set up an orchestra which uses a hundred players for its Carnival performances. The focus is the year's Panorama tune – a calypso chosen by the orchestra, arranged by a resident or guest arranger, learned note by note and phrase by phrase (for few pannists read music), and slowly stitched together over the season.

The Panorama competition, in district and national phases, begins a couple of weeks before Carnival with an all-day preliminary round which attracts virtually every orchestra in the country – often 70 or 80. The national semi-finals with 16 orchestras, and the finals with twelve, are held before an enormously zealous crowd in Port of Spain on the Thursday and Saturday before Carnival, and tremendous prestige surrounds the winner. Though the better bands maintain a repertoire that includes classical and pop tunes as well as calypso (and a small year-round performing team of perhaps 20 or 30), the real test is the ten-minute arrangement prepared for Panorama, a complex overture delivered *fortissimo* throughout, full of cascading runs and trills and split-second virtuosity, calculated to provoke a crowd to an ecstacy of excitement. Some of the bands play on the streets on Carnival days and attract a crowd of supporters and pan-pushers who help to wheel the instrument racks along.

Mas' Camps

Carnival proper is dominated by masquerade (mas') bands, the largest of which may have 3,000 or 4,000 members, led by the top-rank band designers and organisers like Peter Minshall, Edmond Hart, Raoul Garib, Stephen Lee Heung and Irvin McWilliams. Early in the season, sketches of the various costumes are displayed at the *mas' camp* (band headquarters) and masqueraders sign up to book their choice – by the mid 1980s, TT$250–350 was a common price range. The band adopts a theme for the year, which could be something from history, from mythology, from nature,

from fantasy, or something drawn from local cultural tradition. The band is presented in sections, each representing a different aspect of the theme. It also has a king and queen and often several 'individuals' as well, all seasoned masqueraders with large elaborate or dramatic costumes. Rank-and-file masqueraders often have little more than a tunic and boots together with a simple headpiece and standard. In some bands, women outnumber men by as much as ten to one . . .

To *play mas'* is to join a masquerade band and plunge into the action. Carnival Monday. now tends to be a warm-up day, with many bands below full strength and masqueraders only partly costumed. Carnival Tuesday is the big day, with bands in full colours moving between competition sites from early in the morning often until well after dark. By the mid 1980's there were five sites in Port of Spain, the main one at the Grandstand of the Queen's Park Savannah, the others in city squares. Judges later name the Band of the Year in large, medium and small categories, and spectators at the Savannah also name their own 'People's Choice' by voting at the end of the day.

During the Carnival season, mas' camps are fairly used to visitors coming to see how costumes are made (but don't interfere with the work). And it is worth looking at the traditional Carnival skills which include wirebending (for the big costume frames), bootmaking, working in aluminium and plastic, and copper-beating (for elaborate breastplates and headpieces). The large king and queen costumes, which parade in separate pre-Carnival competitions, are the big technical challenge, as they try to combine size, colour and spectacle with lightness and flexibility and the capacity to move. Many are really cunningly designed floats, supported by wheels but propelled and vitalized by the masquerader who 'wears' them.

Old Mas'

This is a simple masquerade, with down-to-earth costumes, often rudimentary, no fuss about colour, and plenty of bawdiness. Old Mas' bands compete in some of the bigger pre-Carnival fetes and dominate the streets during J'Ouvert (see below). They take as their theme some local joke or scandal and function as a series of live, linked cartoons, the caricature figures using placards inscribed with tortuous puns to make their point (first placard: 'Whatever happened to Elizabeth Arden?' Second placard: 'Max Factor').

44

Pre-Carnival Shows

In the week before Carnival, the Savannah plays host to nightly shows, as well as sprouting a Carnival Village at the entrance, which is a good centre for information and daytime diversion. King and Queen competitions, steelband competitions and other events culminate on Sunday night with the Dimanche Gras show, where in recent years the King and Queen of Carnival and the Calypso Monarch have been chosen and crowned.

J'Ouvert and after

The most respectable way of plunging into the Carnival proper is to go to Dimanche Gras on Sunday night, then on to a fete afterwards, and go right through the night and straight into Monday morning. Carnival itself begins at 4 a.m. on Monday with J'Ouvert (pronounced Joovay) – Jour Ouvert (daybreak) – the great pre-dawn procession into town. From fetes on all sides, the bands spill out onto the streets followed by thousands of revellers and slowly converge on the centre of Port of Spain in a slow, euphoric tidal wave of music and chipping feet. The Old Mas' bands are judged in Independence Square, but most people follow their chosen steelband in a hypnotic progress through the throng. For many Trinidadians, J'Ouvert is the real Carnival, forget the glitter to come.

J'Ouvert often lasts until mid-morning, after which some sleep is allowed for those who have been up all night, and the first masquerade bands don't appear till late morning. On Carnival Tuesday, however, everybody is assumed to be fit and fighting; masquerade bands in full regalia are on the road by 8 or 9 a.m. and, in a good year, the action continues well after sunset. In recent years there have been efforts to revive the traditional Last Lap, in which weary revellers took a final jump through the streets in the cool of the night before the official end of Carnival at midnight.

But you don't have to sign up and play mas' for two days if the thought of such exertions appals you. Large crowds watch the action at the competition sites (especially the Savannah), where you get the best idea of what the bands are actually portraying. Many watch in solitary comfort on TV. Or you can simply wander through the streets watching the bands pass by, joining in the wake of now one, now another, for a brief jump-up.

At midnight on Tuesday it all stops; technically, at least. The long season of celebration gives way to the ashes of Lent. Once, in

this Catholic country, that meant no calypso on the radio, ashes on the forehead, something given up, steamed fish on Fridays. Much of that has changed; 'last lap' fetes and 'champions in concert' shows now stretch well into the season of austerity.

6

Carnival's Roots

The original importers of Carnival celebrations were the French planter-immigrants who flooded into Trinidad 200 years ago. To begin with, Carnival was a polite, elegant, upper-crust amusement for the French and Spanish aristocracy, from which black Trinidadians were pointedly excluded; it was a matter of house-to-house visiting, disguises and Cinderella balls.

But with the abolition of slavery in the 1830's, the Carnival rapidly became an Afro-Trinidadian street festival and a heady symbol of freedom. It became a vehicle for satirising and debunking the (now British) colonial élite. The whites withdrew hurt, loudly deploring the festival's effect upon the lower orders and vainly trying to keep the merriment under proper control. But for 60 years the black underclass of colonial Trinidad dominated the Carnival. The press year by year expressed the chagrin of the colonial establishment: 'wretched buffoonery', 'an annual abomination', 'a diabolical festival', 'an exhibition of wild excess'. The authorities reduced the Carnival days from three to two, clamped down hard on the rowdier elements after a series of riots in the 1870's and 1880's , banned drumming in 1883, did away with the Canboulay procession in 1884 – this, the re-enactment of the old slave processions which were called out to deal with the pre-crop burning of the sugar cane (cannes brulées), had by then become the great opening procession of Carnival, with torches, drums and stick-fighters.

But Carnival was too potent an institution to be suppressed even by a police chief as zealous as Captain Baker in the 1880's. We have seen how slave society developed its own underground world, complete with secret hierarchies and rituals. By the 1840's this had surfaced in communal backyard 'tents' of bamboo and thatch which functioned as rudimentary mas' camps, complete with drumming and drum dances, singing and entertainment. These candle-lit, smokefilled sanctuaries were often presided over by a king and queen. The precursor of today's calypsonian was the chantwell, who developed the Carnival songs, rehearsed them and led the community onto the streets on Carnival days.

Out of these tents evolved some of Carnival's traditional figures, many of whom are making a modest comeback today, like the Dame Lorraine, a cartoon figure mocking the white planters and their eccentricities. It was not suppression that eventually began to tame the Carnival bands and set them on the road to today's total respectability: it was probably the element of competition, introduced in the 1890's by a thoughtful Port of Spain merchant anxious to raise the moral tone of things. Today virtually every aspect of the Carnival is competitive, with judges organised by the Carnival Development Committee (CDC). The great Canboulay procession finds its echo in the peaceful J'Ouvert; the traditional figures of Carnival which used to exercise such fascination and power are now the subject of nostalgic reminiscence and conservation lobbies: the jab-jabs and jab mollassies, the devils and bats, the pierrots and tall-stilted moko-jumbies, the Midnight Robber with his convoluted oratory, the minstrels and Indians and sailors.

Calypso

Calypso, inseparable from the Carnival, traces its roots back beyond those city tents to Africa and the praise and satire songs of the West African coast where most of Trinidad's black population once came from. The root name, kaiso, is a Nigerian word. After emancipation, it grafted itself naturally onto the emerging mass Carnival and began to function as a sort of popular press, a source of information and comment and a way of scandalizing the white establishment, as well as providing Carnival music.

Since the turn of the century, steady social change has prised calypso away from its tent setting and into the marketplace. Its French-based patois gave way to English; people started moving from one tent to another to see what was happening; audiences started gathering for rehearsals. Some tents started charging admission: the first organised calypso tent in the modern sense was opened by a railway ticket collector known as Chieftan Douglas in 1921. Improvisation flourished and waned, and with it novelties such as full-scale calypso wars between leading singers, calypso dramas and duets.

Calypso slowly became respectable; one of the great names of the 1940's, Atilla the Hun, was actually a city councillor and deputy mayor of Port of Spain. Calypso kept up its assault on the colonial authorities, who in return maintained their attempts to censor, license or intimidate the calypsonian. Singers became folk heroes, figures full of swagger and machismo, a stance reflected in the names they adopted – Terror, Tiger, Lion, Panther, Striker, Bomber, Sniper, Atilla the Hun, Executor – usually with 'Lord' or 'Mighty' as a prefix.

During the war, the American military provided a new and appreciative audience and indirectly brought calypso face to face with the realities of the international market. Calypsonians had been recording in the United States since the 1930's, but when the Andrews Sisters recorded a little tune called *Rum and Coca Cola* and sold five million copies of it, its creator Lord Invader made not a cent.

The year 1956 brought the PNM to power and gave calypso its greatest practitioner, the Mighty Sparrow ('Yankees gone and Sparrow take over now,' he warned, accurately). Sparrow has more or less dominated calypso since then, though the first ten years were his golden ones: calypso has never quite engaged with society in the same way since, being uncertain of what to make of political change or the oil boom's affluence. Many singers kept under cover with safe themes – Carnival, women, parties, sex; Carnival and Bacchanal became stock rhymes. But Sparrow brought calypso into the modern era, gave the calypsonian status and recognition, fought for acceptance of the art on radio and in business and made a visibly good living out of it.

Like his arch rival Lord Kitchener, Sparrow withdrew from routine competition years ago, and will probably be honoured as Calypso King of the World till his dying day. Kitchener had been singing calypso since Sparrow was a choirboy in his native Grenada; six years before Sparrow burst upon the scene, Kitchener had led an invasion of the sacred turf of Lords cricket ground in London to celebrate a West Indies victory over England. But he still performs with teenage vitality and has a knack of producing good road march

Calypsonian — The Mighty Chalkdust

tunes which sound well on pan.

The abdication of Sparrow and Kitchener opened the way for a new generation which has already become the senior calypso brigade. There was the charismatic Shadow, who defied all convention in 1974 by discarding the obligatory stage caperings and glossy suits and emerging instead in a black cape and a black broad-brimmed hat, jumping straight up and down like a madman, eyes glaring out of a deadpan face. There was Calypso Rose, an earthy, laughing, broadbeamed singer brimming with vitality. There were singers determined to restore lyrics and commentary to their rightful place: the teacher-calypsonian Chalkdust, who picked up the monarch's crown as soon as Sparrow and Kitchener put it down; the tall bespectacled Relator, who won the crown in 1980 with a song urging the then Prime Minister Dr Eric Williams to 'take a rest'; the cheerful Black Stalin who won in 1978 with his classic 'Caribbean Man' and again in 1985. And in their footsteps came younger singers, some from other Eastern Caribbean islands, specializing in jumpy party tunes – Arrow, Swallow, Poser, Scrunter, Penguin, Blue Boy, Becket, Crazy.

In the early 1970's calypso entered a new and probably decisive stage. Led by Lord Shorty – at 6ft 4in the tallest singer in the business and since transformed into Ras Shorty I – leading singers introduced *soca*, a cunning blend of conventional calypso and up-beat American styling. Partly a reaction to social change and as an attempt to package kaiso in glossier clothes for the international marketplace, soca makes the running these days. Shorty claims to have invented it. 'Soca is calypso,' he insisted in a 1979 interview; 'it's the nucleus of calypso, the soul. I felt it needed something brand new, to hit everyone like a thunderbolt. I knew what I was doing was incorporating soul with calypso, but I didn't want to say soul calypso or calypsoul. So I came up with the name soca.'

Tassa drummers. Hosay Festival

So don't be fooled by *Yellow Bird* or *Island in the Sun*, by straw hats or flowered shirts. Calypso today is authentic folksong, with all of folksong's vigour, brashness and cruelty. The calypsonian is a stylish, extrovert artist who – if he's good enough – spends the Carnival season in Trinidad and much of the rest of the year moving between the other islands and the expatriate Carnivals of New York, Toronto and London. Today's calypso is fast-moving, skilfully packaged dance music. And its two traditional functions are still very much alive. The composer – often anonymous and often not the singer himself – either writes a song in which lyrics are vital because they seek to comment, debate, attack, praise or satirize; or a song in which rhythm and melody are the real interest and words are secondary, a tune for moving to. Even the 19th century debates over calypso's decency stagger on in modern disputes over the acceptable degree of 'smut' or calypso's macho approach to women and sex.

Pan

The other great offshoot of Carnival, the steelband (or pan), evolved in the oppressed, depressed districts of Port of Spain where life in the 1930's was tough: in the yards and shacks that crept up the hillsides behind the city, in the streets 'behind the bridge' which marked the border between respectable middle-class Trinidad and the rest.

In a roundabout way, pan was the result of the British attempts to control the Carnival a century ago. The drum had long been the key instrument for Trinidad's African masses; but it unnerved the British and the white élite, who found its language alien and threatening. The drum was banned from the Carnival in the 1880's. Revellers turned in time to an unlikely substitute: bamboo stems, cut and dried and beaten, long five-foot basses thudding on the ground, shorter stems beaten together or with metal.

Used in sufficient numbers and augmented by any percussion to hand, like a spoon beaten on a flask of Dutch gin, bamboo stems produced an acceptable booming music. By the 1930's, metal and iron sounds were being routinely added to these tambou-bamboo bands (tambour-bamboo, i.e. bamboo drum): not only gin bottles but dustbins, buckets, biscuit tins or car wheel hubs.

By 1936, in the hills on the eastern side of the city, the Gonzales Place Band was beating metal objects like gas tanks and learning to cut them to vary the sound. By 1937 the papers were complaining about the 'terrific din' of the metal and tin in Carnival bands. In 1938 a band called Alexander's Ragtime Band swept into the city on Carnival Monday morning from the western suburb of Newtown with a distinctly metallic music. Soon, men like Neville Jules of Hell Yard and Winston 'Spree' Simon of the John John Band were discovering how to play simple tunes on the ends of oil drums by beating small areas of the metal to produce different pitches. The nursery rhyme *Mary had a Little Lamb* was one of the first tunes to emerge.

Carnival was suspended during the war, but experimenting went on in back yards all over the city, and by VE Day in 1945, Trinidad was ready to celebrate with the first rudimentary steel bands. The pans were strung around the players' necks (there is still a competition for these early instruments); their range was small, but the old drumming instinct had found a new outlet. By 1950 'Spree' Simon's recitals included waltzes, rumbas, sambas, foxtrots, and even a bit of Tchaikovsky's *First Piano Concerto*; and the first steelband tours began.

But local acceptance was slow to come. Middle-class resentment was strong and it took courage to stand up and defend pan. But some did, including the politician Albert Gomes and a leading churchman, Canon Max Farquhar, who wrote: 'Instead of succumbing to sullen despair or violent retribution, the panmen turn to the escapism of music and roam our streets, the gay troubadours of a race which traditionally, in the face of adversity, has found relief in dancing and song.'

The older band names conjure up those early struggles: Desperadoes, Invaders, Renegades, Casablanca, Tokyo. The aggressive overtones recall a time when panmen really were desperadoes and renegades and when belonging to a band meant accepting a fierce, gang-strong loyalty. When steelbands clashed then, broken heads were the result; there was none of today's official and international acclaim. Now, there are middle-class pannists, women pannists, Chinese, Indian and white pannists; the newer bands carry gentler names – Birdsong, Nu-Tones, Silver Harps, Pan Groove. Warfare is confined to Panorama, and there is little hostility left (though a good deal of indifference outside the Carnival season, a neglect

The 'sweetness' of the pans is the pan tuner's business

much resented by the pan movement during its nine-month off-
season).

Today's bands are of a size and sophistication that would have
seemed impossible in 1945. At Panorama, the 200–300 pans (the
name applies to the instrument as well as the music and the culture)
are mounted on mobile steel racks. The transformation from industrial waste to concert instrument is the business of the tuner who
produces the pans, tunes them and gives the instruments their
distinctive tone. The first thing most tuners do is beat one end of
the oil drum into a concave shape with a sledge-hammer. On this
surface the notes are marked out and slightly raised. Most of the
drums have to be cut: only the basses, with the lowest notes, stay
intact.

There are several main sizes of pan. The very shallow pans are
the tenors, producing the highest, melody line, corresponding to
the first violins of a conventional orchestra. Below may come,
according to each band's custom, double-tenors (two pans mounted
side by side, providing a wider range); altos or double-seconds
(again double-pans but with a lower pitch, like violas); the guitars,

pitched at about the range of horns and trombones; and then the bigger pans – cellos, tenor-basses and basses (perhaps six full drums to a player). In the middle of it all, keeping the rhythm on which the whole group depends, is the rhythm section, which will probably include a conventional trap set but also an array of beaten metal – cymbals, scratchers, old brake drums. The rhythm gives the music its distinctive vitality and surge, producing cross-rhythms so complex that Western musicians have trouble unravelling them. The pannists use sticks to beat the pans with, often tipped with sponge balls (or the intestines of golf balls) for the bigger pans, or rubber (perhaps derived from the handles of hockey sticks or cricket bats, inner tubes or simply rubber bands) for the higher pans.

After cutting the pan to size and marking out the notes, the tuner heats it over a fire and tempers it with water or oil. Then the real tuning begins, each note being worked over with hammer and chisel until the pitch is secured. Tuning is a continuous job: before a big performance, the tuner will spend a day retuning and blending a band's intruments – rough handling, constant movement and changing temperature all affect tuning.

There is still no standardized design or concert pitch for pans: tuners design their own instruments, so a pannist transferring from one orchestra to another may have a new spread of notes to master. Veteran tuners, like Tony Williams or Bertie Marshall, bring real acoustical precision to pan design: Williams's 'spider web' design, named after the way the notes radiate from the centre, was the result of observing how certain notes sound clearer when placed next to certain others.

A panyard waits for the evening practice session to get under way

Steel orchestras now play everything from classics to soul – many pannists say they like playing classics because it stimulates stick technique and ensemble and broadens experience. Outside Panorama, the big showcase for pan is the Steelband Music Festival, held in the National Stadium in alternate years: there, each orchestra has to perform a classical test piece (recent choices have included work by Handel, Mozart and de Falla), and a classical work of their own choice as well as a calypso arrangement or local composition. Slowly, the movement is evolving original music written for the instrument: leading names to look for in that area are Len 'Boogsie' Sharpe of Phase II Pan Groove and teacher-pannist Ray Holman.

In the panyards during the Carnival season you will find an intense concentration. Few players read music and the arranger often has his arrangement in his head or in sketch form, developing it as he goes along. Early rehearsals are thus a matter of each section learning and practising its own part; the total concentration on the pan itself builds an enormous rapport between players and allows a split-second precision, every stick connecting at the same instant without any conductor's baton as a guide.

Later, the whole band will concentrate on a phrase or section, playing it over for what seem hours on end until it sounds right; only after several weeks is the whole tune put together, interrupted only when something goes wrong. Through the middle of all this strides the captain or arranger, shielding his ears against the main sound to focus on a particular section or player; his imperious rapping on the edge of a pan is the sign to start or stop.

The pannists of Trinidad and Tobago are perhaps the only musicians in the world with the satisfaction of belonging to a movement – and playing an instrument – that was painfully evolved out of immediate experience by themselves, their fathers and brothers, and in places familiar to every one of them. Their panyards are not hard to find in the Carnival season – follow your ears or ask directions to the best known centres. Outside the Carnival season, you may have to seek out pan music at certain fetes and hotels and occasional concerts. Recordings of pan are slowly reaching high technical standards – pan, like the organ, is notoriously difficult to record well, but you should be able to pick up albums by leading orchestras like Desperadoes and All Stars and maybe recordings from recent Steelband Music Festivals.

7

People

Little is left of Trinidad and Tobago's earliest settlers, the Amerindians, except a series of lyrical names: Guayaguayare and Chacachacare, Naparima and Mucurapo, Carapichaima and Cunaripo, Tacarigua and Tunapuna – some of the places as sweet as their ancient names, others not. A small Carib community with its queen survives near Arima.

Not a great deal more is left of the long, precarious Spanish presence. Pastelles and parang music are essential to a Trinidad and Tobago Christmas, though both may have more to do with Venezuela than with Spain. There is a good deal of Spanish blood left, but again the most visible legacy is names: Santa Rosa and Santa Cruz, San Fernando and San Rafael. The last sad remains of the Illustrious Cabildo can be tracked down on Sackville Street in Port of Spain, behind a dreary, crumbling facade.

The British legacy has provided Trinidad and Tobago with its formal face: the English language, the legal system, Parliament and the constitution, a fondness for jackets and ties, and a sense of propriety that asserts itself in the oddest ways – in the midst of the Carnival bacchanal there will suddenly be a furore about scantily clad women dancing for the TV cameras with what is considered an undue sensuality, or about an indiscreet level of smut in somebody's calypso.

But Africa and India more or less decide how things are done beneath the surface, exercising a powerful influence on religion and food, music and dance and styles of living; while France and Spain underpin the French-based patois that is still spoken and the dialect which everybody uses when not in formal situations. 'Perhaps the epitome of a Trinidadian,' wrote novelist Merle Hodge, 'is the child in the third row of the class with a dark skin and crinkly plaits who looks at you out of decidedly Chinese eyes and announces herself as Jacqueline Maharaj.' And it is not only the Amerindians and the Spanish who have left their footprints on the landscape. Apart from Caroni and Tamana, Manzanilla and El Socorro, a casual drive may bring you to Blanchisseuse or Grand Riviere, Brighton or Scarborough, Fyzabad, Bombay Street or Cawnpore Road.

Today's population of around 1.1 million is made up mostly of descendants of the Africans who were brought to the islands as slaves, and of the East Indians who followed them after emancipation. The 1980 census put these groups at 40.8 and 40.7 per cent of the population respectively, and since the Indian community has long recorded a faster growth rate it is virtually certain that by the mid 1980's Indo-Trinidadians were the largest ethnic group. Whites, mainly descendants of the Frenchmen who poured into Trinidad from 1783 and the British families who settled in both islands during the long period of British rule, represented only 0.9 per cent of the population in 1980. The Chinese community accounted for 0.5 per cent and other groups – of Portuguese, Middle Eastern or other ancestry – for 0.8 per cent. 16.3 per cent were classified as mixed.

It is a youthful population, with over a third aged 15 or less, and one that has enormous vitality and exuberance. Writers have sometimes puzzled over this, wondering why these particular islands should produce more energy and invention and individualism than their neighbours; they tend to conclude warily that Trinidad's late start, its brief period of slavery and the immediate dilution of the population by immigrant groups from all over the world gave it a unique sense of experiment and rootlessness which has flourished rather than wilted with the years. That might account for the tenuous connection many Trinidadians feel with the land, the sense of camping or passing through, and for the compensation of a particularly sensitive nationalism. But, be that as it may, the fact is that Trinidad and Tobago is one of the world's great polyglot societies; and, unlike other well-mixed people, those of the United States for example, the population had taken its present form by the middle of the 19th century, and has had time to settle into a coherent society in which tensions, though not absent, are understood and controlled.

The net result is intriguing. There have been times when it looked as if the only way Trinidad and Tobago's population could become one people would be if the Afro-Trinidadian, creole, largely Westernised culture became the norm, and everybody else fitted into it. To some extent that has happened – but the norm has been stretched steadily wider. By the mid 1980's, one of the most respected pan arrangers was Indian, from an old French village with Spanish cultural traditions. Indian tassa drums were appearing in Carnival bands, Africans had got quite used to joining the Hindu and Moslem festivals of Phagwa and Hosay, and a senior Cabinet minister of Indian descent was regularly standing in for the Prime Minister and quietly challenging the old taboo about Indian political power.

Trinidad and Tobago still has a rich stock of ethnic stereotypes:

Phagwa, the Hindu spring festival: not just devotions . . .

Africans are supposed to be lazy, spendthrift and prone to feteing; Indians are supposed to be suspiciously hardworking, prone to violence and despair, and cunningly successful in business; Chinese are supposed to control laundries, restaurants, corner groceries and whe-whe games.

There is a rich line in cheerful ethnic insults; Indian programmes still occupy sacrosanct blocks of time in the TV and radio schedules; and there is still an acute awareness of the degree of people's whiteness (there is black, black-black, brown, light-brown, high-brown, red, off-white . . .). The Indian community continues to be perceived as a minority when it is statistically a majority. These things can still spark off deep feeling: but by and large they are treated with good humour, and the underlying insecurities are weakening.

Festivals

One result of so much diversity is a lavish menu of public holidays and festivals to ensnare the businessman and divert the visitor. Quite apart from the Carnival, which overshadows the first three months of the year, the Hindu community celebrates several religious festivals, the main ones being the spring festival of Phagwa or Holi, and the festival of lights, Divali.

Phagwa, which has taken on overtones of a carnival itself, is the start of the Hindu new year and is preceded by a season of several weeks; it coincides with spring in India, and has been observed since the first Indian immigrants landed in Trinidad in 1845. During the season, singing groups in villages and temples perform *chowtal* songs, music which – though religious – is bright and gay and concerned with the renewal of spring. It is accompanied by *dholak* (hand drums) and *jhaal* (small brass cymbals). A huge bonfire on the eve of Phagwa symbolises the victory of light over darkness and good over evil, and in hectic festivities the following day, *abeer* (coloured water) is cheerfully thrown over everybody within reach, including Trinidad and Tobago's President who frequently attends.

The main Phagwa ceremonies can be found in March on the Aranguez Savannah on the outskirts of eastern Port of Spain, as well as smaller sites throughout the country. In the (Indian) autumn comes Divali, a haunting and beautiful festival closer to the

Christmas of the Christians. It begins the festival of Ramleela, and conjures up the great Indian epic, the Ramayana, and Ram's return home after rescuing his wife from the evil Ravanna. At night, thousands of *deyas* – flickering candles in earthenware crucibles – are lit and placed on paths, walls and windows to light the way for the returning hero.

The smaller Moslem community also has two major festivals: Eid-ul-Fitr (which like Divali is a public holiday) and Hosay. With Carnival-like overtones of its own, Hosay or Hosein attracts a growing non-Moslem following: it commemmorates the death of the Prophet Mohammed's descendant, Hussain, in AD 680, and marks the end of the month of Muhurram. The street processions carry *tadjahs* – beautifully decorated replicas of the tombs of Hussain and Hassan which are worked on for weeks beforehand – to the accompaniment of tassa drums, and are led by dancers twirling on their shoulders enormous effigies of the moon. Like Carnival costumes, the *tadjahs* are discarded at the end of the festival, being cast into rivers or the sea. The Port of Spain suburbs of St James and Tunapuna are good places to see this festival. Later in the year, Eid-ul-Fitr marks the end of the month of fasting, the great month of Ramadan, with the sighting of the sliver of new moon in the evening sky.

The major Christian festivals are observed as holidays – Christmas, Easter, Whitsun, Corpus Christi; so are Labour Day (June 19, Uriah Butler's great day), Emancipation (August 1, replacing the Discovery Day holiday that used to mark Columbus's landing), Independence Day (August 31) and Republic Day (September 24).

Towards the end of the year, the major folk festival – the Prime Minister's Best Village Competition – takes up residence at the Queen's Park Savannah in Port of Spain. It grew out of political meet-the-people tours in the 1960's, but now takes in virtually everyone and everything: suburban as well as village communities, traditional cooking and crafts, folk dance and song, village decoration and hygiene. The hour-long village concerts are one of the best ways of getting a feel of traditional everyday life; the performances include folk singing, dance, and a drama which is often ingeniously constructed to weave all the required ingredients into a single story line. Thus you can lurch suddenly from spirituals or folk songs into a stately French bélé, back to calypso, on into a Spanish or Indian or even Chinese dance, back into a waltz, sideways into

The Roman Catholic cathedral in Port of Spain was finished in 1832, when its site still overlooked the sea

the Christmas music of parang . . . The result is a parade of Trinidad and Tobago's memories and dreams, stereotypes and prejudices, grace and vulgarity, humour and pathos, all integral to a folk culture which is thus rescued, not always virginly intact, from a slow underground death.

Religion

You might say unkindly that the Carnival is Trinidad and Tobago's real religion, the thing that is taken most seriously of all in people's lives. But that would be unfair. About a third of the population is Roman Catholic, thanks to the long French and Spanish presence. About 15 per cent is Anglican, thanks to the (perhaps less persuasive) British: 3.9 per cent are Presbyterian (the church which made real inroads into the Indian community through Canadian-staffed missions in the late 1000's and early 1900's, creating a large group of Westernised Indians with unmistakably respectable accents). Among the Indian community, Hinduism accounts for 25 per cent

A new mosque at Mucurapo: reminder of the strength of the Muslim community

Hindu temple on Ethel Street, St James: a quarter of the population is Hundu

of the national population, and Islam for 5.9 per cent. Another 16.6 per cent was classified in the 1980 census as 'other', a term that covers a large number of fringe churches with often very devoted and vocal followings, including the Ethiopian Orthodox, the African Methodist Episcopal, the Baptist Union, the Church of God, the Church of the Nazarene, the Church of the Open Bible, Jehovah's Witnesses, Seventh Day Adventists, the Unity Church, the Open Bible Standard Churches and the Methodists; while the radio stations are loud with stout-lunged American evangelists and their local disciples.

Being inseparable from the broader culture of language and society, Islam and Hinduism function as powerful cohesive forces for the Indian community. There are particularly well-known mosques at St Joseph, San Juan and on Port of Spain's Piccadilly Street, and an easily-found temple at Ethel Street in Mucurapo; but these are the tip of the iceberg. Outside Hindu homes across the country, fluttering coloured flags on tall bamboo poles (*jhandis*) tell of the *puja* (thanksgiving or prayer) ceremonies in progress – red for the god Hanuman, yellow for Lakshmi or Durga or Krishna, black (rarely) for Kali. The *puja*, conducted by the saddhu or pundit, is the centre of both religious and social life.

But perhaps the most intriguing of all religious realities in Trinidad and Tobago is the survival of African faiths, virtually hidden beneath the surface of conventional society. Several African traditions took root during slavery, of which the major survivor is the Yoruba tradition from what is now Nigeria. Its forms of worship survived a century and a half of proscription, and remain identical in many aspects to surviving ceremonies in Brazil and Haiti, Cuba and Nigeria. In Trinidad and Tobago, the presiding deity (*orisha* or power) is Shango; the ceremonies take place in unobtrusive compounds, in a tent or small house known as the palais, which may be a temporary or permanent structure with room for drummers and dancers on one side. There is a consecrated area where the shrines and implements of the *orishas* are kept; outside are other shrines called stools, and coloured flags on bamboo poles. There are flowers, candles, incense, the smell of sacrificial food; everything is spotlessly clean.

The priests (*mogbas*) wield real power and responsibility over their spiritual children, and include many women and at least one prominent Indian. During the ceremonies, spiritual fervour is

64

whipped up by dance and drumming, leading to the manifestation of one or more *orishas* in the persons of chosen worshippers, who become for a while possessed and take on the known characteristics of the *orisha*. The dance is enormously vigorous and skilful, particularly after possession has begun; the *orisha*, far from invoking evil powers or black magic, is asked for guidance or solace, to heal, or simply to preside over a ceremony in his or her honour. Among the *orishas* called upon are Ogun, the warrior god and patron of war, hunting and iron; the dancer moves as if doing battle. The dancer possessed by Shakpana will take a cocoyea (palm branch) broom and begin vigorously to sweep. Oshun, the graceful goddess of rivers and lakes, moves gently, swimming or rowing, bathing or combing her hair. Shango himself, the god of thunder and lightning, moves with violent and powerful steps, often using fire. Yemonja, the mother of the *orishas*, is the protector of sailors and fishermen; Obatala turns his vehicle immediately into a trembling, aged figure who hurries to don white robes, dances with slow laborious steps, and becomes a moving symbol of great spiritual power.

This ancient worship has acquired overtones of Christian and even Hindu belief in an intriguing example of syncretism. African *orishas* are frequently identified with Christians saints – Ogun with the archangel Michael, Shango with St John. The patron saint of the south Trinidad village of Siparia, La Divina Pastora, is recognised by Hindus as Sooparee Mai and worshipped in the same way – and she is one of the powers manifested in the palais (the Siparia festival takes place two Sundays after Easter). This book will not offer directions for tracking down this African tradition, since casual outsiders, not necessarily sympathetic, may not always be welcome. But sensitive observers can with a little determination find someone to take them to the right places.

Language

Like most of the Caribbean, Trinidad and Tobago is in a loose sense bilingual. There is a formal English which is used in formal situations, in education and writing, in school and government (well, usually). There is an informal English, variously called a dialect or a second language, which is used in everyday situations, between friends, in homes and bars and offices; it is basically English but with a distinctive vocabulary and structure. It finds parallels in most Caribbean islands and of course in England's different counties, all of which have their own accents and intonations and structures.

The main difference is that much of Trinidad and Tobago's informal language comes from older forms with deeper roots in France, Spain and Africa. The common language of 19th century Trinidad, below the white élite, was a French-based patois, a language evolved by the slaves out of their languages and borrowings from the languages of their masters. Patois is dying out now, and is little spoken except by older people in the country districts; though in islands with a stronger French presence, like St Lucia, it is still in common use. Occasionally you might still hear Spanish in Trinidad; you can certainly hear Hindi. And the language is inevitably being agitated now by a transfusion of American (especially Afro-American) words and intonations.

The Trinidad and Tobago dialect is imperceptibly in retreat: time-honoured phrases and idioms begin to date and sound stilted. But it is not a difficult language once your ears are tuned – though it is very hard to use accurately unless you grew up with it. Among common words and expressions the visitor may encounter (many obviously of French origin) are the following.

Liming is the art of spending time in the most relaxed way with friends and without strain – drinking, talking, watching the girls go by; it produces the noun *lime*. A *fete* is really a lime *par excellence*, as we have seen, and can be virtually a fulltime profession. *Steups* or *cheups* is an attempt to record the sound made by sucking the teeth, or more accurately clicking the tongue in the English way but making a much juicier and more lingering job of it. It expresses disgust, exasperation, frustration or goodhumoured disagreement, and is possibly the most common sound in the whole of Trinidad and Tobago. *Horn* is used in the sense of Shakespeare would understand, applied both to the activities of the unfaithful spouse and the plight of the betrayed partner (the calypsonian Blakie had a calypso, delivered with mouth-watering relish, entitled *De Horner-man Come*, i.e. watch out for your wife). Not unconnected is *maco* (noun or verb), i.e. minding somebody else's business.

The language is rich in terms of mockery and abuse. *Picong* or *fatigue*, to *heckle* or *mamaguy*, all have to do with poking fun at someone, and can all have pretty painful barbs attached. To *mauvais-langue* or *bad-talk* is to speak ill of someone, usually with malice aforethought. A *cunumunu* is a dolt; a *mamapoule* is a weak or effiminate man. *Maljo* (*mals yeux*) is the evil eye; a *pappyshow* is a laughing-stock; someone who's *basodie* is drunk or confused or both.

Some apparently familiar phrases acquire new meanings. *Just now*, for example, means 'hold on' 'coming in a moment' or 'some time soon'. *One time* denotes a surge of optimism and decisiveness ("I'm going down to the lawyer's and settle everything one time"). *Fuh so* (for so) indicates a degree of awe and relish: 'is going to be fete fuh so' or (perhaps with reference to a satisfying traffic accident or fracas with the police) 'it was bacchanal fuh so'.

Superlatives, spurning conventional grammar, are often established by repetition – pan music is not simply sweet but sweet-sweet-sweet. (Cf. to *back-back*, meaning reverse.) Going *up the islands* means travelling north up the Eastern Caribbean chain, which is inhabited by 'small islanders', while going *down the islands* means a trip to Trinidad's offshore holiday islands like Gaspar Grande. A *lagniappe* is an extra bonus, tough luck suggests that *crapaud smoke yuh pipe*, a *bad john* is anyone whose air of general worthlessness is matched only by his display of machismo. But if defeated or confused by all this, it's normally safe to spread your arms, raise your eyes helplessly to heaven, and say *But look mih crosses* . . . It should raise a laugh at least.

Folk Tradition

Like everyone else's, Trinidad and Tobago's folk tradition is slowly being lost, despite the Best Village Competition and the revivalists. But there have been several tactical victories. There has been some success in restoring traditional characters to the Carnival: each has its own dance movement, and it may be possible to see King Sailors, Firemen, Moko Jumbies, Devils, Dragons and Imps, Burroquites, Bats, Indian and African Warriors and even Tobago Speech Bands in the Carnival for a few years yet.

Many of the traditional folk dances are found mainly on the Best Village stage now. They range from the graceful French *bélé* and *piqué* and the Spanish *joropo*, *manzanares*, *parillo* and *castillan*, through Indian dances such as the Moon dance of Hosein, the *Ghatka* (stick dance), *kollatam*, *jharoo* and Fire Pass, to the African dances for the *orishas*, bongo dances for the dead, traditional African nation dances and the Tobago Reel and Jig. There are burlesques on the fringes of the old-time Carnival, like the Dame Lorraine poking fun at portly colonial matrons, or the Police and Thief dance; there are variations of stately British dances like the Quadrille and Jig, Reel and Lancers. There are children's game dances (like *Brown Girl in the Ring*) and work dances. Whether the *limbo* originated in Trinidad and Tobago is not really clear, though it seems probable: this standby of Caribbean hotel cabarets, in which a dancer bends back into a horizontal position and dances beneath an ever-lowered (and often flaming) bar, was presumably a dance to show off male prowess and agility. In some parts of the country you can still see the *Kalinda* dance by the traditional stick fighters.

Dance in Trinidad and Tobago conjures up the name of Beryl McBurnie, who in her pioneering Little Carib Theatre almost single-handedly forced a psychological change and brought real Caribbean dance into the open and onto the public stage in the 1940's and 1950's, when all local art forms were considered inferior, by definition, to the foreign product. It is a battle that still has to be finally won.

On the Best Village stage, too, you may catch sight of the legendary figures which haunt the folk imagination. There is the *soucouyant*, who sheds her skin in the night and flies through the dark as a ball of fire to suck the blood of her sleeping victims. A circle of rice around the bed is an advisable protection, since she has to stop and eat it, or a dose of salt on her discarded skin. The *douen* is the spirit of an unbaptised child, which lives in the forest, raids your garden, and lures away living children on moonlit nights. You can recognise a douen because its feet point backwards; it wears a straw hat and a long plait. The *Diablesse* is easily recognised too, for she wears a big hat and hides her one cow-foot under a long frock. She frequents cemeteries and cross-roads, where she seduces men with her beauty; but at the crucial moment she turns into a hog and the deceived man plunges down a precipice. Two sticks crossed over the chest can ward her off. The *Jack-a-Lantern* is a light that appears in the night to lead you astray, particularly if you are an old lady on the way to Midnight Mass, while the *Lagahou* is really the obeah-man or medicine man disguised as an overgrown pig. More benevolent spirits are *Papa Bois*, the protector of animals and guardian of the forest, who is half man and half animal; and *Mama d'l'eau*, the goddess of the river.

Like the rest of the Caribbean, Trinidad and Tobago has always known about the medicinal properties of plants, and you can still get advice on which plants can be brewed into bush tea to relieve any specific complaint, including flu, fever, malaria, hypertension, diabetes, diarrhoea, pneumonia, venereal disease, indigestion, arthritis, toothache, convulsions, dropsy, athlete's foot, asthma, worms and snake-bite. Man-better-man, for example, known to scientists as *achyranthes indica*, is good for flu and has a proven expectorant action. Wild coffee (*cassia occidentalis*) is a useful purgative, while Bellyache Bush (*jatropha gossypifolia*) is a good emetic and Fowl Foot (*eleusine indica*) is used against diarrhoea.

Parang

Just as Carnival means calypso and pan, so Christmas means parang, the Spanish-Venezuelan music that takes hold of Trinidad and Tobago in the weeks before December 25, even if Bing Crosby goes on roasting his chestnuts on his open fire. The word probably comes from *paranda*, a spree or lime, and the music's home is the valleys of St. Ann's and Santa Cruz, St. Joseph and Caura, and towns and villages with a strong Spanish legacy, like Mausica, San Rafael, Rio Claro, Lopinot and Arima.

Traditional parang means a group of musicians and singers moving from home to home, being rewarded for their music with food and drink. The songs are in Spanish with lively rhythms, and deal with traditional Christmas themes. The *paranderos* use guitars, cuatros, maracas and shac-shacs, mandolin and violin, bandola and tiple. The primary form is the old Spanish carol, the *aguinaldo*, followed after suitable refreshment by the *joropo* and *castillan*, the *guarapo* and *manzanares*. Since the war, though, there has been less house-to-house visiting, and parang is heard more at parties, on the radio and in competition.

8

Diversions

Homes and Buildings

Along the western side of the Queen's Park Savannah in Port of Spain there is a line of proud mansions which one architect, John Newel Lewis, christened the Magnificent Seven. They were built in the early years of the century by wealthy local families, their exuberant tangle of styles and aspirations reflecting the diversity of the nation's roots. At one end is the austere Stollmeyer's Castle, built by a family from Germany, modelled on Balmoral Castle in Scotland and called Killarney by Mrs Stollmeyer who wanted to go

Stollmeyer's Castle, one of the 'magnificent seven' overlooking the Queen's Park Savannah in Port of Spain

Queen's Royal College: where V. S. Naipaul and Dr Eric Williams went to school

Landmarks of the oil boom: twin towers of the government's Financial Complex

to Ireland at the time: a bizarre vision of turrets and battlements looking out onto the peaceful Savannah. At the other end is Queen's Royal College, the Anglican boys' school which trained novelist V. S. Naipaul and Dr Eric Williams: it is in mock German Renaissance style, topped off with a lighted tower and chiming clock. The Catholic Archbishop lives in one of the intervening mansions, the Anglican Bishop in another, the Prime Minister has his office in a third. In the middle stands the most bizarre and extravagant of all, Roodal's Palace, whose cupolas and domes would credit a French chateau. 'Larger than life, bold, daring, singular,' wrote Newel Lewis, 'they sing out the individualism characteristic of the country.'

Few buildings in Trinidad and Tobago are more than 150 years old – the two cathedrals in Port of Spain are among a handful of exceptions. The rigours of tropics and termites, damp air and withering sun, not to mention the ravages of fire and demolition, have seen to it that a building's life span is normally modest. The Amerindians came to terms with this by evolving an easily constructed, easily expendable house, the *ajoupa*: with a frame of branches, a roof of palm thatch and a finishing of clay, it could be put up in a day or two and was cool, dry and airy. Latterday variations can be seen all over Trinidad and Tobago, in the vendors' stalls of Port of Spain and urban centres, or the old chattel-houses of working people – wooden, resting on concrete bricks for support, theoretically moveable, roofed with galvanised iron.

Each successive wave of arrivals in Trinidad and Tobago sought its own balance between the sensible *ajoupa* and memories of metropolitan architecture. The French built lofty, airy estate houses with high, steep roofs, high ceilings and white fretwork boarding, which proved cool and dry. As a merchant class developed, it built two-storey town houses – living and sleeping quarters upstairs, stores and warehouse space downstairs, with ornate iron balconies on slender supports; some can still be seen. The Victorian era brought with it a taste for decoration and ornamentation: elaborate roofs, filigreed galleries, turrets, dormers, crestings, finials, fretwork. Jalousies became the universal answer to the ventilation problem; eaves grew broader as the fear of hurricanes eased, and verandahs began to sneak right around the house for privacy and coolness. Ceilings were kept high, often with a space above the walls to help air to circulate; houses climbed off the ground on stilts, not merely to evade snakes, insects and floods, but to look taller.

The result is a legacy of wholly distinctive buildings: you can still find good examples of these 19th century estate houses, grand town houses, ornate middle-class homes with gingerbread fretwork. Some have suffered conversion into offices, sometimes with taste and skill, often not. And with the rapid growth of the middle class in the last three decades, newer variants have evolved in the mass housing of Port of Spain suburbs like Diego Martin or massive estates like Santa Rosa near Arima, where potentially soulless concrete structures have been rendered individual and exuberant by additions, protuberances, decorations, green lawns, sculpted burglar bars and extravagant stereos. Though as these houses grow larger, as at Valsayn, so they have tended to look inward, retreating into airconditioning and carpeting behind security fences and growling Dobermen.

In the same way, the newer public buildings show the influence, not of Paris or Madrid, but of New York and Miami, smart concrete boxes pretending that the warm air and sea breezes are non-existent, sealing themselves off from the outside world. Trinidad and Tobago is proud of its large modern structures, like the twin towers of the Financial Complex on Independence Square, the Hall of Justice overlooking Woodford Square, or the government offices of the Riverside Plaza; but they are a more radical departure from the *ajoupa* than the country has ever attempted before.

Sport

A great deal of national energy goes into sport, and a third of the nightly television news is devoted to recording the results. There is a fine new National Stadium at Mucurapo on the edge of Port of Spain, which can handle all the major sports to international level. American influence in the Caribbean has not yet persuaded Trinidad and Tobago to take up baseball, American football or (to any great extent) basketball; but it plays hockey, netball, football and rugby, runs marathons, jogs endlessly (the Savannah is a favourite course), warms to boxers and wrestlers, flocks to keep fit and master martial arts. An average year has 52 horse racing days in Port of Spain, San Fernando, Arima and Tobago.

In season you can hunt anything from armadillo to alligators, including agouti, wild hog, lappe and deer, so long as you have a

National Stadium, Port of Spain

licence. There are more yachts in the harbours near Port of Spain and San Fernando than you can count, and there is good fishing, both inshore and in deep water, including kingfish, Spanish mackerel, snapper, barracuda, marlin, grouper and bluefish – June to October is the best time for trolling. There are excellent scuba and snorkelling sites in Tobago; there are tennis courts at the Trinidad Hilton, public courts in Port Spain and some of Tobago's hotels, and 18-hole championship golf courses at Mount Irvine in Tobago (an idyllic setting under the palms) and at Moka near Port of Spain, as well as a public 9-hole course at Chaguaramas and several other courses from Brighton to Balandra. Tobago even offers goat racing and crab racing, particularly on Easter Tuesday.

But perhaps the one great passion above all others is cricket, whose season is the dry season, January to May. When the local or West Indies team is playing, do not be surprised to get no response from people in the office or on the street, because they will have a transistor against the ear. The writer C. L. R. James, whose great specialities are cricket and politics, observed that the African slaves must have been indoctrinated into the game by their masters, probably as fast bowlers. Cricket has long been a deadly serious matter at any level above the beach game, and often there too; each village traditionally had its club and pitch, and there was deadly rivalry between different national clubs, as there is now between the Caribbean islands which contest the annual Shell Shield regional championship (though more relaxed fete matches are also a favourite way of passing public holidays). The Oval ground in Port of Spain, with the hills of the Northern Range as a backdrop, is a beautiful spot to spend a very Caribbean day if you have the chance.

The Arts

Carnival and its attendant arts of calypso and pan take up the real energy and attention of Trinidad and Tobago, to some extent sucking the vitality and validity out of the more conventional arts – which often seem to be searching for a role, for things to say which match the statements of Carnival. Some of the country's best writers, for example, have long since settled abroad, including V. S. Naipaul, Samuel Selvon (the author of wry comic novels), C. L. R. James, playwrights Errol John and Errol Hill. But novelist Earl Lovelace has stayed at home and his books are well worth looking for. Among earlier work which laid the foundations for a national literature are the novels of C. L. R. James, Ralph de Boissiere and Alfred Mendes. Look too for the novels and history of

The Queen's Park Oval in Port of Spain is one of the world's great cricket centres

Michael Anthony, the dialect poetry of Paul Keens-Douglas, and Merle Hodge's novel *Crick Crack Monkey*.

The dance is perhaps the most vibrant of the conventional arts; it has more to draw on in the way of folk roots, and forever tries to balance its nationalism with the techniques of modern black American dance. The theatre, however, is still trying to find a form that fits national experience; its most successful products have been musicals, combining dance and music with a tough script, such as *The Joker of Seville* by the St Lucian poet and playwright Derek Walcott (who is regarded as Trinidadian by adoption, since he founded and, for 15 years, directed the best theatre group of the time, the Trinidad Theatre Workshop). There are many theatre companies, which produce some interesting work, but the formal techniques of metropolitan theatre do not mesh easily with the volatile national psyche, and many productions feel uneasy as a result. The group which has had most success in popular terms is the Strolling Players, led by Freddie Kissoon, who writes and directs the plays: they travel widely, attract large audiences, and deal mainly with the stock humour of everyday life. Apart from the Queen's Hall in Port of Spain, which doubles as a community centre, the capital has two theatres – the intimate Little Carib, and the Astor, a converted cinema, both in Woodbrook.

Thanks to some devoted teachers and a biennial Music Festival (with professional adjudicators from Britain and thousands of participants), 'classical music' flourishes. There are some particularly good choirs – the Marionettes Chorale, for example, has won honours at recent international choral festivals, and sings a vast repertoire ranging from baroque liturgical music through pop songs and Broadway to spirituals, Carribean folk song and calypso. The Opera Company has staged *The Magic Flute* and *The Marriage of Figaro*, *Carmen*, *Die Fledermaus*, *Cavalleria Rusticana* and *Pagliacci* with local singers and orchestra. The Music Festival has nurtured some excellent pianists and singers, some of international stature like Jill Gomez and Sandra Browne, and there is a small concert society – the Recital Club – which stages monthly concerts by local and visiting artists.

For a while in the 1970's it looked as if Trinidad and Tobago was going to develop a film industry. After a series of tongue-in-cheek thrillers – *The Caribbean Fox*, *The Right and the Wrong*, *Operation Makonaima* – an American film-maker, Hugh Robertson, arrived in

Trinidad with his Trinidadian wife and made *Bim*, a film of real substance. But financial obstacles prevented a follow-up, and that promising avenue remains deserted. The advent of video on top of television has dealt a death blow to commercial cinemas, not so much in terms of quantity – in 1985 there were still over 40 – but of quality, with exhibitors apparently unable to find an audience for international releases.

The oil boom years of the 1970's and early 1980's produced a small class of art collectors, and a handful of art galleries opened up, including Art Creators in St Ann's and Art Mart in Diego Martin. The visual arts, too, have fought a long struggle against metropolitan perceptions, a struggle to see what is actually there and render it in a style that can match the Carnival or the Magnificent Seven for distinctiveness. The first real Trinidad artist was Jean Michel Cazabon, who was born in Port of Spain in 1813, and left an invaluable body of work, much of it watercolour landscapes of the Trinidad of his time. There is a permanent exhibition at the National Museum and Art Gallery at the top of Frederick Street in Port of Spain (which in 1985 was being restored and revived). Among other names to watch for are Alfred Codallo, Sybil Atteck, Noel Vaucrosson, Edwin Hing Wan, Pat Chu Foon, Dermot Louison, Boscoe Holder, LeRoy, Clarke, Pat Bishop and Jackie Hinkson.

Leisure

Because Trinidad and Tobago never developed a large tourist industry, leisure activity and nightlife, like sport, are integrated into national life, and provide few tourist enclaves. The country has always repelled casinos, and there is little night-clubbing in the conventional sense. The hotels have their floor shows and cabarets, the Hilton has its Aviary Bar and the Holiday Inn its Calypso Lounge. Most of the sleazier clubs and floor shows of the sixties and seventies have disappeared, and the discotheques have taken over the scene. One leading name is JB's at Valsayn, which has a good restaurant attached; another is Atlantis in the West Mall outside Port of Spain. In Tobago the best known name is Club La Tropicale near Scarborough. But there is no shortage of good watering holes both in the towns and beyond: nearly all are primarily for local

The Queen's Hall, Port of Spain: theatre, concert hall and community centre

communities and clients, so don't expect tourist facilities. Quite a few pub-style bars have opened up in recent years, including the Cricket Wicket opposite the Oval in Port of Spain, Spaniard's Inn (in Victoria Avenue) and the renovated Pelican (Coblentz Avenue, St Ann's).

Media

There is one government-owned television station, with two channels, and a number of private television production houses all trying to sell material to it. Applications for a second station have never been approved. There is one government-owned radio station (Radio 610) and one privately owned station, Radio Trinidad, a subsidiary of the British Rediffusion group. Both run FM channels as well as mainstream AM programming.

There are two morning papers, the tabloid *Express* and the broadsheet *Guardian*, which each sell 50,000 to 60,000 copies a day; Sunday editions go to 90,000–100,000. Each produces an evening paper – the *Sun* and the *Evening News* respectively. There is also an array of weekly papers, ranging from the serious to the entirely flippant; they include the *Catholic News*, the *Mirror* (twice a week), the *Bomb* and the *Sunday Punch*. A highbrow *Trinidad and Tobago Review* appears from time to time and the *Naturalist*, the country's only surviving glossy magazine, dedicated to wildlife and the environment, appears nine times a year.

9

Food and Drink

Live crabs: essential ingredient for Sunday callaloo

Whatever it thought about cricket, Trinidad and Tobago did not take too kindly to the cooking of Old England, and British cuisine has left little mark on national eating habits in spite of – or because of – 165 years of exposure. In fact there is no such thing as a national cuisine except in the sense that many dishes are creole: for Trinidad and Tobago eats virtually everything that has been developed or imagined by the many people who have settled there, except Yorkshire pudding and steak and kidney pie. You may be eating standard international fare one day, hot Indian curry the next, followed by creole pelau, French black pudding, bacalao (saltfish buljol), Chinese char-sue pork and Spanish pastelles. The key to cooking, as to so much else, is diversity. Among the few (almost) constant factors are rice, which has become a universal staple; lavish spices and seasoning; and hot pepper sauce, which is applied to everything.

This diversity is reflected in the choice of restaurants. There are plenty of Chinese restaurants which may offer little in the way of romantic ambience but are usually up to the mark in the kitchen. Oddly, there are few Indian restaurants, though you can often find small, unobtrusive ones, particularly in central Trinidad. In Port of Spain and the main towns there is a choice of places – often small converted homes catering more for lunchtime business than dinner – which concentrate on creole food in relaxed surroundings. And there are restaurants which offer good standard international menus, sharing the widespread Caribbean belief that many tourists can only eat steak and chips, but sometimes embellished with unusual specialities like Polynesian food.

But the best place to explore national cooking is in people's homes, if you can contrive to do that, and the best times are the festive times – Christmas, Carnival, Eid-ul-Fitr (which like Easter is supposed to break an arduous fast). The presence of a large Indian community means a sizzling array of good curried meats and vegetables, cooked as they would be in India rather than as exotic diversions for the jaded palates of metropolitan diners, and mixed with dhalpouri (ground split peas) or paratha. Non-Indians may yet have to come to terms with Indian movies and music, but they have embraced Indian food with enthusiasm. One of the most popular forms is the roti, which is eaten either as a meal or as a takeaway food: this is curried beef, chicken (often with the bones removed), potato, liver, goat, vegetables or shrimp, folded inside a soft dough wrapping. A variant of the dough is often served as part of a meal and known as buss-up-shut.

What tends to make people delirious with nostalgia for home, however, is creole cooking, which traces its roots back to the Amerindians and Africans, but has absorbed useful lessons along the way from France, Spain, Venezuela, the Middle East and the Mediterranean. Among the most hallowed dishes are:

Pelau or peas-and-rice, cooked with meat (chicken or beef) and peas, often flavoured with coconut (which is used in a range of stews and soups) and a little pepper (peppers are customarily placed whole into the pot to give off a little heat and flavour without bursting, so mind you don't swallow one).

Callaloo, which like pelau is also found in other islands, is made of the green leaves of the dasheen bush, together with ochroes (okra), boiled up with pumpkin, coconut, salt meat like pig's tail or fat pork, and pepper. Crab and callaloo is a classic Sunday lunch speciality.

Souse is pig's trotters and tail, boiled and served cold in a salty sauce with lime and cucumber, pepper and slices of onion.

Buljol is shredded saltfish mixed with onions and tomatoes, avocado, pepper and olive oil.

Sancoche is a soup made with salt meat, root vegetables, dumplings, leftovers and coconut milk.

Blood pudding or black pudding is highly spiced blood sausage.

Apart from these delicacies, there is a good tradition of seafood (especially in Tobago, which helps supply flying fish to Barbados): lobster, shrimp, crab (and crab backs), snapper, conch, kingfish. The Chinese make deep-fried wantons out of shrimp, and there is a fresh water fish, the cascadura or cascadou, which (legend insists) will cause you to end your days in Trinidad once you taste it. One thing the country has which will not be found in the other islands is wild meat such as agouti, manicou and tatoo, for which creole cooks reserve special time-honoured treatments.

The original fast food: coconut milk and meat on sale by the Savannah

Sorrel, basis of the essential Christmas cordial

Then there is a whole range of minor delicacies. One sacred ceremony, for example, is to go to the Queen's Park Savannah of an evening for a bite to eat, and sample the supplies of the vendors around the sidewalk. There are oysters, plucked from the roots of the mangrove in the coastal swamps outside the city, which can be licked out of their shells or seasoned with a little pepper, ketchup and vinegar – though the oyster vendors were having a little trouble with the public health department at the time of writing and may not reappear, vindicated, for a while. But there is still roast corn, barbecued over a coal-pot, and there may be shark-and-bake, served up hamburger-style, boiled corn with pig-tail, or roti. There are sure to be coconuts: the vendor slices off the top with a swish of his cutlass, and you simply drink down the sweet water inside. After that, you can scoop out the white jelly with a sliver of shell sliced into a makeshift spoon by the cutlass. Like most sacred ceremonies, the Savannah pilgrimage for oysters, corn and coconut water is not as obligatory as it used to be; some vendors have taken to refrigerating their coconuts as an extra attraction, which seems to many customers an offensive piece of progress, particularly since it pushes up prices. But the Savannah still has a strong flavour of the essential Trinidad. Roti can of course be found in stalls and outlets in most parts of the country, though the young set tends to favour the ubiquitous chicken-and-chips outlets and the nests of fast food counters, including pizzas, that the shopping malls have spawned.

Other dishes to try? Sure. Cowheel soup; ice-cream made of soursop, granadilla or barbadeen, guava or coconut; tamarind balls; coconut bake, homemade sweetbread; sugar cake; tullum (grated coconut, molasses and sugar, sold by wayside vendors); doubles (curried channa in stretchy cornmeal dough); guava cheese (really a sweet – guava pulp sold as sticky sweet squares). Creole cuisine makes good use of tropical fruit and vegetables: breadfruit (roasted, fried or stewed), plantains (like bananas but cooked as vegetables, sliced and fried, or boiled and mashed into balls as foo-foo), avocadoes (known as zaboca), bananas, pumpkin, pawpaw (served with a slice of lime and a much better breakfast starter than cornflakes), soursop (which makes a marvellous tangy punch), guava, yams, sapodilla, pomerac, citrus.

There are several sorts of mango, all of them succulent. A Trinidad journalist once told me scathingly how he saw a celebrated novelist eating a mango *with a spoon and fork*: the withering contempt for such fussy respectability reflects the belief that a mango, to be eaten properly, must have the teeth sunk into that glorious, orange flesh so that the juice runs down your chin and along your arms. Otherwise, clearly you haven't really experienced the mango.

Christmas is probably the height of gourmandising in Trinidad and Tobago. It demands a large ham, traditionally home-cured and certainly home-cooked; turkeys and chickens; and plentiful pastelles, the Spanish patties made of seasoned mincemeat mixed with olives, capers and raisins and wrapped in corn-meal casing, then packaged in banana leaves (arepas are similar but fried). Christmas is also the time for ginger beer, sorrel (red and sweet, brewed from the flowering buds of the sorrel plant), and ponche a crema, a thick

Angostura bitters, first produced to soothe the turbulent stomachs of Simon Bolivar's revolutionary army, are found world wide

83

creamy cocktail made of eggs, rum and sweetened condensed milk and served with crushed ice.

Oddy, Trinidad and Tobago is hard up for good fruit juices, in spite of having so much fruit; it actually imports fruit juice and juice concentrate, so that fresh orange or grapefruit or passion-fruit juice is harder to get than in a Miami hotel. Like other islands, however, it does produce good mauby, the tangy drink with aniseed flavour brewed from tree bark. Try also sea moss, which is brewed from seaweed and more pleasant than its origins might suggest (many islands make excellent beer from seawater, after all, and you could never tell . . .).

Trinidad and Tobago of course makes some of the finest rum in the Caribbean, which means in the world; it is generally lighter rum than that of its older competitors in Barbados and Jamaica. Rum is often taken straight by serious groggists, perhaps in a small shot washed down with water, or from a *petit quart* in a rum-shop. It is also mixed with water or soda, a sweet mixer or the ubiquitous coca-cola, legacy of the US military presence during the war. But for a mix you won't easily find in many other places, try coconut water as a mixer for rum or gin.

In the last few years, the rum companies have begun producing their own gin, vodka and rum punch, and there is a pleasant coffee liqueur, Mokatika, reminiscent of Jamaica's Tia Maria. Trinidad and Tobago is also the home of Angostura bitters, which were first concocted over 160 years ago in Venezuela by a young Prussian army surgeon in need of something to settle the turbulent stomachs of Simon Bolivar's revolutionary army. The blend of herbs, spices and plants which the young Dr Johann Siegert developed is still the basis of today's bitters, which are found in every self-respecting bar and kitchen in the world, and are used to season cooking, brighten up cocktails, pinken gin, and still quieten restless stomachs.

Siegert, having made his formula into a business, moved to Trinidad in 1875, escaping political upheaval in Venezuela, and re-established the business there; his three sons – Carlos, Alfredo and Luis – gave their names to familiar suburban streets in Wood-brook. Siegert's great-grandson copied out the secret formula in 1963, cut it in four and posted the four quarters separately by registered mail to a New York bank vault. In Trinidad, only four men are supposed to know it, and they won't travel on the same plane together.

10

Wildlife

A giant leatherback turtle, two metres long, heaves itself out of the dark Atlantic waves. It eases itself up the beach towards the high tide line, where in the dry sand it will lay its eggs, perhaps as many as a hundred, before crawling slowly back to the water. It may do this four times or more during the mating season – from about March to September – before disappearing for another year into the deep ocean waters.

Several miles away, in the limestone caves of the Northern Range, a colony of oil birds is stirring, preparing for the nightly foraging expedition among the fruits of the mountain forest. They fly through the pitch dark cavern using an echo-sounding navigation system like the bat's, but audible as a series of sharp, high-pitched clicks.

Many countries can point to mysterious, moving sights and events in their natural life, and Trinidad and Tobago is no exception: the flocks of Scarlet Ibis flying home to roost in the mangroves of the Caroni Swamp at sunset, the bat caves of Mount Tamana, sightless fish, fishing bats, the unique golden tree frog found at the summit of El Tucuche, the almost extinct bush turkey or pawi.

But what makes Trinidad and Tobago unusual is the range and diversity of its natural life. Until about seven thousand years ago, Trinidad was part of the South American mainland, and was separated only by the rising of the ocean level after the ice age. But that ancient continental link has left mainland as well as island life forms crowded into a small area. It has mountainous rain forest, mangrove swamp, seashore and savannah all close to each other. It is a major crossroads on the migration paths of birds moving north and south. Its savannah is an extension of the *llanos* of central Venezuela; the northern range is a continuation of one branch of the

Deer are among the many wild creatures living in Trinidad's forests

great South American cordilleras, and rises above 3,000 feet into elfin woodland at El Tucuche (3,072 ft) and El Cierra del Aripo (3,085 ft). Most of the rest of Trinidad is flat or gently rolling country, except for the smaller Montserrat Hills in the centre and the Trinity Hills in the south. Tobago, now much closer in character to the Windward Islands further north, was probably joined to Trinidad and South America in the much more distant past, though there is some puzzling evidence of an independent mainland connection as well. Only a sixteenth of Trinidad in size, it is more uniformly hilly, except for the flat southern end, its mountainous spine rising to well over 1,500 feet.

Partly because of this ancient continental past, Trinidad and Tobago now supports over 600 species of butterfly, over 400 species of birds, and over 2,000 different flowering plants. The sheer diversity – a total of 100 different mammals including bats, and 70 different reptiles, including lizards and snakes – has made the islands a serious attraction for naturalists, and particularly ornithologists.

The evergreen and deciduous forest is the home of wild animals like the agouti, paca (known locally as lappe), armadillo (tatoo), opossum (manicou), deer, and peccary or wild pig (quenk), all of which are hunted; also of the tayra (chien bois or wild dog), ocelot (tiger cat) and anteater. Further afield, hunters prey on the Amazon parrot, iguana, duck and heron, plovers and sandpipers, though there is official protection for some species, like the howler and capuchin monkeys.

There are only four poisonous snakes in Trinidad and Tobago, all rarely seen. Two are pit vipers – the mapepire zanana or bushmaster, and the mapepire balsain or fer-de-lance. The other two are coral snakes, one larger than the other, both with beautiful red, white and black rings. The many other species are non-poisonous, though there are four boas, including the anaconda and the common boa, known as the macajuel – the anaconda, living in the swamps, can swallow a six-foot alligator.

Lizards like the ground lizard or zandolie are common, as are the many geckos, including the white wood-slave which lives indoors, often hiding behind pictures on the walls. It is entirely harmless and friendly, but much feared, perhaps because of its clinging tenacity on walls and ceilings – folklore is full of warnings about the dire fate that will overtake you if a lizard jumps on you. The largest of the lizards, looking like a miniature dinosaur, is the iguana, which grows to six feet (including the tail) and is entirely vegetarian. Frogs and toads abound, particularly in the wet season, and you will hear their raucous calls all over the islands. The butterflies include the wonderful iridescent blue Emperor, while the 20 or more freshwater fish include the cascadura, whose ominous powers have been referred to already, and the guppy, which was first identified in Trinidad a century ago by an ichthyologist called Lechmere Guppy, and is known locally as millions.

Perhaps it is the birds which are the biggest curiosity. There are 400 species in Trinidad, more than anywhere else in the Caribbean, and 150 in Tobago. Many are annual visitors, either escaping

The Caroni Swamp, on Trinidad's west coast

The Scarlet Ibis, Caroni Swamp's famous resident, one of the two national birds

the northern winter or avoiding the colder months at the other end of the globe by leaving the southern region of South America between May and September to winter in Trinidad. But many are permanent residents, including many South American species not found elsewhere in the Caribbean. The most common have become so familiar, even in towns and suburbs, that they are known to most school chidren – like the yellow tails or corn birds with their nests like long narrow sacks, or the antics of the bluebirds or the blueblack grassquits, called Johnny-Jump-Up because of the male courtship rituals conducted on branches or power lines, involving much squawking and excitement.

Tradition insists that the Amerindians called Trinidad Iere or Kairi, and that this meant 'land of the hummingbird', though it may simply have meant 'island.' But there are at least 16 hummingbird species; many are forest residents, but they also regularly visit gardens to feed and sometimes nest there. Brown pelicans and laughing gulls are inescapable companions at the beach, swooping for fish: also, very often, are the black hooded corbeaux scavenging around the day's catch. The kiskadee – named for its cry, which is translated as *qu'est-ce qu'il dit?* – is heard every where, even in Port of Spain, and is really a yellow and brown flycatcher. Other familiar characters include the longtailed mockingbird, known as dayclean, and the ruddy ground dove, called zortolan.

Observation Posts

About 20 miles from Port of Spain, 1,200 feet up in the forested hills on the road to Blanchisseuse, is a good place to start coming to terms with this profusion: the Asa Wright Nature Centre on the Spring Hill estate, an old estate house whose verandah peers through the forest down the long lush Arima valley, is a natural observatory, equipped with feeding tables and comfortable chairs. On the Centre's grounds is the only easily accessible colony of night-flying oil-birds, or guacharo (the Venezuelan Spanish word meaning one who laments, a reference to the dismal screams the birds set up when they are disturbed; locally they are also known as diablotin). These normally inaccessible birds roost and raise their young in several caves in Trinidad and in northern South America, but only here have they made the mistake of choosing a site within easy human reach. The cave, formed by a stream cutting through limestone rock, is a fairly easy walk from the house.

The centre is also a hotel, with basic, even spartan conditions, but with some old-world comforts too: tea is served in the deep leather armchairs of the verandah. There are nine nature trails around the Centre and well-organised expeditions.

The Caroni Bird Sanctuary on Trinidad's west coast is the next major site, and the place to see scarlet ibis. The sunset flocks returning to roost are smaller these days, and sometimes do not materialise at all; the ibis are no longer breeding in the Swamp, perhaps because of the disturbance of hunters and rowdy trippers, or the overhead flight path of aircraft approaching Piarco airport. To breed, they have retreated to the Venezuelan coast and the quieter islands of the Orinoco delta. But there are still plenty of birds roosting in the Swamp, and their dawn and dusk movements are still a moving sight. And the Swamp is in any case a mysterious, tranquil place; a trip through it in the company of a good guide is an experience. Apart from the ibis, there are pelican, egrets, herons, plover, duck, sandpipers, rails, spoonbills.

The Nariva Swamp, 15,000 acres of freshwater swamp draining into the Nariva River and fringed with palm forest, lies on the Atlantic side of Trinidad. It has red howler monkeys, alligators and anacondas, four-eyed fish, yellow-hooded blackbirds, orange-winged parrots and elusive red-bellied macaws. Here the Suriname toad raises its young in pockets on the female's back, and the paradox frog grows to nine inches as a young tadpole before shrinking to two-and-a-half inches as an adult frog. In central Trinidad, the Aripo Savannah is a remnant of the Venezuelan savannahs and retains bizarre life forms like the bladderwort and the sundew, plants which trap and digest insects, as well as ground orchids found nowhere else in the world.

Tobago has two bird sanctuaries, on the offshore islands of St Giles and Little Tobago. St Giles is the most important seabird breeding colony in the southern Caribbean, but landing is difficult; there is a fine range of species including the frigate bird or man o'war, the red-footed and brown booby, and Audubon's shearwater. (There are 13 official wildlife sanctuaries in Trinidad and Tobago, ranging from the Caroni Swamp and El Tucuche to the Soldado Rock off Icacos Point, where sooty and noddy terns breed, and Saut d'Eau near Maracas Bay, Trinidad's only pelican breeding area.)

The tall immortelles once shaded cocoa and coffee crops

The Chaconia (wild poinsettia) is the national flower: named after the last Spanish governor

Little Tobago is easily reached from the village of Speyside. Sometimes known as Bird of Paradise Island, it was the place where, in 1909, 50 Birds of Paradise were brought from New Guinea to the western hemisphere when it was feared that large-scale poaching would make the birds extinct. It didn't. In Little Tobago's 450 acres the birds adapted well enough, but never stood up to the occasional storms, and their numbers dwindled over the years; it is assumed that there are none left now.

Elsewhere in Tobago, the lush gardens of the Arnos Vale Hotel are one of the main centres for birders: afternoon tea there is something of a ritual, as mot-mots (king of the woods), woodpeckers, tanagers and other birds gather for a meal of coconut and fruit while visitors sip their tea and watch. There are underwater coral gardens just offshore, and leatherback turtles sometimes nest on the beach right in front of the hotel. The other place to go is the Grafton Estate, where the late Mrs Eleanor Alefounder devoted much of her life to creating an environment where birds would feel free to come and feed and where visitors could relax and watch. There is no accommodation at Grafton, but there are trails and distant views of the seas.

Another interesting site for the birdwatcher is the Pointe a Pierre Wildfowl Trust, on the compound of the Pointe a Pierre oil refinery in south Trinidad, a valuable nature reserve where endangered wildfowl species are bred. The Emperor Valley Zoo in Port of Spain, beside the Botanical Gardens just north of the Savannah, is probably the easiest place to see a sample of the country's natural life: named after the big Emperor butterflies found in many parts of Trinidad including the Emperor Valley, the zoo has a large collection of monkeys as well as snakes, deer, wild pig, armadillo, ocelot and anteaters.

Behind the Zoo, the islands' most spectacular tree has given its name to Poui Hill: visitors in the dry season may be able to carry away a memory of the brief, two-or-three day flowering of the poui trees which splash the hillsides with vivid yellow and pink. The old saying is that the poui must blossom three times (some say twice) before the rain begins. There is a particularly fine example in the grounds of the Country Club in Maraval. There are several fine trees around the Savannah on the northern fringe of Port of Spain, providing welcome shade, with the cassias, for strollers and joggers and covering the ground with a brilliant yellow carpet of blossom for a few days after their swift and spectacular flowering. On the western edge of the Savannah, opposite Queen's Royal College, is one of the finest specimens of the unusual cannonball tree to be found anywhere. And two other trees which add a welcome stroke of colour in the dry season are the African tulip and the immortelle, which once shaded cocoa and coffee crops and whose red mist of bloom is best seen in January and February.

Everywhere in the two islands there is a rich variety of flowers as well: parks, open spaces and private gardens are bright with red amaryllis lilies, yellow allamanda, and red and yellow and white hibiscus. Many homes are surrounded by hedges of small red hibiscus and Turk's cap, or the massed small blooms of the bougain-villea. The national flower is the chaconia, with its distinc-tive horn-shaped red blossom; named after the last and greatest Spanish governor, Chacon, it blossoms in late August, around the time of independence. And any time is a good time to seek out another of Trinidad's curiosities: the mud volcanoes of south Trinidad, which are really small quasi-volcanic mud flows. The most accessible site is the Devil's Woodyard east of Princes Town, though there is less activity there than there used to be. Further, south, near Palo Seco, is a mud glacier, and the Moruga Bouffe offers an almost lunar landscape where the mud rises four or five metres high. For an interesting woodland environment, seek out Cleaver Woods, near the Eastern Main Road, just west of Arima.

11

Port of Spain

It's as well to get your bearings to start with, so begin by climbing up to Fort George.

When the British seized Trinidad from Spain in 1797, the great fear was that Spain or some other power would try and snatch it back again. Thus as soon as the island was formally ceded to Britain, the Governor set about defending it. On the foothills behind the city, Governor Hislop built a series of gun batteries – remnants of some, including the restored Fort Picton, can be tracked down on the Laventille Hills. Already there was a sea defence, Fort San Andres, which then stood off the waterfront (now it is ignominiously occupied by the traffic police on South Quay). High above the city, Hislop built a fort on Cumberland Hill – where the television transmitter is now – and just below that he placed the major defensive position, La Vigie, later known as Fort George, which commands the sea approaches to Port of Spain and the opening through the Dragon's Mouth to the open sea.

Little remains of the fort now, except bits of the guard house and the cells, and the heavy cannon peering out towards the Gulf, initialled with the insignia of King George. In times of panic, Port of Spain merchants would sweat up the hill to lodge their records, documents and cash at the fort. But they need not have worried; Fort George never saw action, and was demobbed in 1846. Until 1964 it was used as a signal station, its little wooden cabin designed by a West African prince whom the British had drafted into the Public Works Department in the 1880's.

The point of starting at Fort George however is not a further historical expedition in a land blessedly free of obligatory historical sites. It is the view, the same view that made Hislop place his cannon there. From 1,100 feet, you can look down over the whole

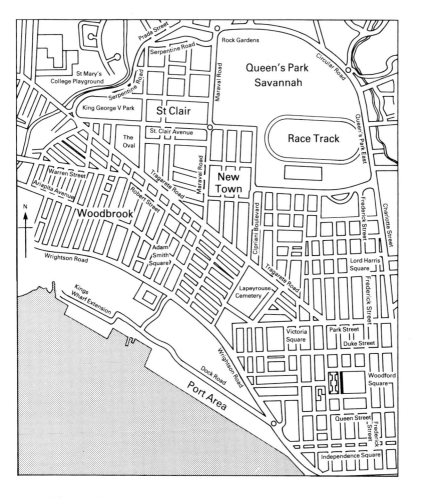

Port of Spain – Street Plan

Port of Spain, from the Lady Young Road

of Port of Spain and the coastline of Mucurapo, scene of the early bloody clashes between Spain and the Amerindians, and the waters where the Spanish were later to fire their own ships in the face of the British advance – now they are dotted with freighters waiting for berths in the Port of Spain docks. To the east, the hills of the Northern Range unfold in a series of valleys and spurs, with the hills of Laventille curling protectively around the city's flank. Beyond are the flat sugar plains of Caroni and, misty in the distance, the Montserrat Hills and the outcrop of Mount Tamana. On a clear day you are able to see right down the west coast past the Caroni Swamp and Point Lisas and the refinery town of Pointe a Pierre to the San Fernando Hill and the Cedros peninsula on the horizon.

Directly below Fort George, on the other (western) side, is the crowded valley of Diego Martin, Port of Spain's biggest dormitory suburb. Beyond, the Northern Range hills stretch to the very tip of Trinidad, where Venezuela lies just across the narrow and turbulent Dragon's Mouth. In the distance are the high mountains of Venezuela's Paria peninsula, while nearer are Trinidad's offshore islands – the prison island of Carrera, the quarried Kronstadt, Gaspar

Grande or Gasparee, Monos and Chacachacare. There are still better views of Trinidad higher in the hills, but reached only with exertion: you can reach Fort George by driving up the steep and narrow road from St James in less than ten minutes (the road is marked with one of the Tourist Board's yellow and black signs – 'To Historical Site' – as you leave St James heading west, just before the flyover). Beyond Fort George, the road goes a little higher towards Cumberland Hill, but you need a sturdy four-wheel-drive vehicle; better still, walk it.

Port of Spain

Fielding's Caribbean guide finds Port of Spain the most fascinating capital in the Caribbean, but it looks at first like a disaster area, at least from the planning point of view. It seems to deny that it has any relationship with the sea, since the waterfront is virtually closed off; you can see the masts and funnels of vessels at berth, but you have to climb to the upper floors of the nearby Holiday Inn to see them coming or going. Port of Spain is cleaner than it was in the 1970's, but still gives the impression that its people prefer disorder to anything resembling urban planning. Many of the older buildings have fallen victim to fire, old age or developers' bulldozers; there have been some tasteful restorations, but many middle-aged buildings are in a state of advanced decrepitude, as are some of

The Queen's Park Savannah: Port of Spain's lungs and playground

the roads and streets. Parking is almost impossible, and busy tow-trucks known as wreckers eagerly cart away badly parked vehicles without making any dent on the general congestion. Handsome new buildings, imposing edifices of concrete and tinted glass, artificially lit and cooled in the bright sunlight, tower over nearby shacks and stores and rumshops and thickets of overhead power lines. A dozen different tints of rusting galvanised roofs are the city's emblem.

Yet Port of Spain also gives the feel of a living, lived-in city, a disorganised, defiant, chaotic, complex organism that insists on going its own way regardless of planners' norms and the anxieties of metropolitan environmentalists. Although the city centre has lost much of its life as expansion and congestion forces people into the suburbs, its own suburban districts are living communities whose borders you can cross unmistakeably between one electricity post and the next.

On the eastern side of the city centre are the predominantly Afro-Trinidadian suburbs, spreading along the foot of the hills and up the hillsides, the areas where pan was born and where the city's heart beats. These are largely 'behind the bridge', beyond the Dry River into which the St Ann's River was diverted by the last Spanish governor. The main community is Laventille, best seen by driving up Laventille Road from Piccadilly Street, through a maze of homes perched on the steep hillside. On the top of the Laventille Hill, the main landmark is now the church and shrine of Our Lady of Fatima, to which generations of Catholic schoolchildren have toiled once a month during the annual devotions that last from May to October.

Further to the north is the suburb of Belmont, made up of a maze of narrow lanes and the city's first real suburban development – it was settled after emancipation by Africans, many of them freemen, who called the area Freetown. On the northern side of Port of Spain, north of the Savannah, are situated the mainly middle-class suburbs of St Ann's and Cascade, reaching up into the hills along the St Ann's River; Maraval in the adjoining valley to the west; and the upper-crust suburb of St Clair. On the west of the city are the suburbs settled by older middle-class families: St James, which now accommodates a large Indian community, Woodbrook, and Newtown.

The Savannah

The pride and joy of Port of Spain is the Queen's Park Savannah, 200 acres of open land, fresh air and breeze lying between the city and the hills. It is the city's great recreation ground. Here the biggest Carnival competitions take place, and horse racing has its premier track (you can see the horses exercising there in the early morning). Joggers jog round the Savannah, people play cricket and football and exercise and fly kites on it, the city's finest houses look over it, poui trees explode into blossom round its edge, vendors of coconuts and oysters and roast corn patrol its perimeter. In recent years the Savannah has become perhaps the world's biggest round-about, with all traffic circling clockwise around it instead of tangling endlessly at each corner.

Port of Spain owes the Savannah to its first civilian governor, Sir Ralph Woodford, who arrived there as a young man of 29 in 1813, five years after most of the city had been flattened by fire. He arranged to buy land from the Paradise estate of the Peschier family (who reserved a small cemetery site in the middle for their descendants to be buried in) and land from the Hollandais estate adjoining it to the north. Starting out as an open pasturage, the Savannah grew into a gigantic park and playground, the city's lungs. For almost half a century until 1950, a pleasure tram clattered round the $2\frac{1}{2}$-mile perimeter; Trinidad's first aircraft flight took place here in 1913.

In the Savannah's north-west corner, the land dips suddenly into an area known as the Hollows, which has been landscaped and is the site of occasional pan concerts. Across the road is the Emperor Valley Zoo and the Botanical Gardens, also laid out by Woodford (or rather Woodford's gardener) with specimens from all over the planet. Woodford also remodelled the old Peschier estate house and made it the governor's residence; it stood a little forward from the present President's house next to the Botanical Gardens, which was built in 1876 and rebuilt after a fire in 1938. The Prime Minister's house, a newer stone building dating from 1959, lies hidden among trees and shrubs behind that of the President.

From the St Ann's roundabout at the north-east corner of the Savannah, a road named after Lady Young, wife of the governor of 1937–42, snakes up into the hills, past the entrance to the Hilton Hotel, and joins the Eastern Main Road and the Churchill-

The President's House, overlooking the Savannah

Roosevelt Highway at Morvant, a useful short cut for drivers heading east; along the way is a lookout with particularly good views over the city (another can be found up Lady Chancellor Road, which begins just opposite the Hollows). The Hilton overlooks this corner of the Savannah; built on the hillside, on the site of an earlier government house, it is upside down – i.e. you enter on the top floor and take the lift down to the rooms. The poet Derek Walcott once referred to it in a poem as 'this arse-upward Hilton', an unkind phrase he later revised; in fact the hotel is well used by Trinidadians as well as visitors.

On the south-east corner of the Savannah, next to Memorial Park, is the National Museum and Art Gallery, a fine and newly restored building which was opened in 1892 and rebuilt after a fire in 1923; in the mid 1980's it was being revived as a museum and gallery almost from scratch under a new administration.

Downtown

Leaving the Savannah, you plunge into the city. Head south from the Museum down Frederick Street, the main street, past the old

State Prison (formerly the Royal Gaol) on the right, across the east-west Park Street, until you come to Woodford Square, where the late Dr Eric Williams staged many of his famous rallies. This square was also Governor Woodford's doing. When he arrived it was called Place des Armes, a marshy open area through which the St Ann's River had flowed. Woodford bought it, had it planted with rare trees, and was the moving force behind the erection of a new Anglican Church on the south side to replace the old wooden church which had disappeared in the fire of 1808. The Cathedral of the Holy Trinity, which now overlooks the square, was the result: it

Frederick Street, in downtown Port of Spain

was finished in 1818 and consecrated in 1823. There is an impressive monument to Woodford inside, where the original pulpit stood; the Governor's State Pew, where leading colonial dignitaries were expected to worship, was over the north door. There is a fine roof, copied from Westminster Hall in London, supported by mahogany beams and carved in England; and there are six fine stained glass windows above the altar.

On the far side of Woodford Square is the enormous administrative building known for obvious reasons as the Red House. The original was put up after Woodford's time, in 1844–48, and was burned down in 1903 in angry demonstrations over water rates in particular and colonial administration in general. It was defiantly rebuilt in the same pretentious neo-Renaissance style and reopened in 1907. The Parliamentary chamber is in the north wing, and has a startling ceiling of Wedgwood blue and white gesso. On the north side of the Square stood some of the old city's finest houses, all of which have now disappeared, giving way to the big modern Hall of Justice.

Frederick Street leads on past two oddly contrasting shopping areas: on the left is a makeshift vendors' mall, a miniature community with a maze of streets and shops which developed after a large area was burned down in the mid 1970's; while on the right and in the block beyond are the city's leading conventional stores, spilling over into nearby cross streets and into Independence Square. In recent years some of the interest has moved away from this main shopping block into suburban malls, like the Long Circular Mall in St James (which is neither long nor circular – that is the name of the road it's on) or the West Mall beyond St James. Trincity, Chaguanas and San Fernando also have new malls.

When you reach a roundabout encircled by honking taxis and jostling cars, you are in Independence Square. The thoughtful gentleman contemplating the scene from a pedestal with an air of faint distaste is Captain Arthur Cipriani (see Chapter 4), one of the early pioneers of the movement towards independence. The square used to be a long tree-lined avenue called Marine Square, and was one of the earliest parts of the city; the little village of Puerto d'Espana at first consisted only of the eastern end of this square and three streets going northwards Calle de Principe (now Nelson Street), Calle de Infante (Duncan Street) and Calle de Mercado (George Street). It was Woodford who began a long process of land reclamation south of Marine Square and laid out the present South Quay.

From Frederick Street, Independence Square stretches westwards towards the docks and Wrightson Road, the highway leading west out of the city. This section is sometimes called, with a touch of irony, Bankers' Row: it has the Central Bank and the modern towers of the government's financial headquarters. To the east, it leads towards the Roman Catholic cathedral, whose foundation stone Woodford also laid in 1816, though it was not finished till 1832. It is dedicated to the Immaculate Conception, and is built of local Laventille stone and timber in neo-Gothic style. The twin turrets on the western front were damaged by an earthquake in 1825 before the church was finished, and were replaced in wood. It was the first church in the country to be equipped with a computer organ, installed in 1979.

Beyond the Cathedral is Tamarind Square, where the Spanish built their original church, so that it is really the heart of the old town. At the far end, Christopher Columbus, blue-robed, looks down from his own pedestal at developments in the island he called Trinity. Beyond, a highway links Independence Square with the two major roads heading east out of the city – the Eastern Main Road and the Churchill-Roosevelt Highway – which it joins near the main Port of Spain market.

12

Trinidad

The North-west Peninsula

The north-west tip of Trinidad, the Chaguaramas peninsula, is a lovely, wild, fertile area, with the open sea to the north, the Gulf of Paria to the South, and a spine of forested hills between. During the war, it was occupied by the Americans on a long-term lease, the result of a deal with Britain in which some aged American destroyers were swapped for base facilities in the Caribbean. But after the war, Chaguaramas became a sensitive nationalist issue; in 1960 Dr Eric Williams led a march through the rain from Port of Spain demanding Chaguaramas back as the site for the new capital of the West Indies Federation.

But, having got Chaguaramas back, Trinidad never quite knew what to do with it, and today much of the peninsula is as the Americans left it. The Chaguaramas Development Authority has put up huge signs saying 'Cherish Chag', but only a fraction of its own plans have come to fruition. In spite of that, or perhaps because of it, Chaguaramas is a popular playground within half an hour of Port of Spain.

As you drive westwards from the city through Bayshore and Carenage, the road squeezes itself between cliff and sea, past a series of small bays. The rusting metal cylinders which you pass on the right at one point were the floats and weights for the nets which were set to catch wartime German submarines. Just past the old American checkpoint at the entry to the base, the road broadens into a dual carriageway for a hundred yards or so: on the left is an artificial beach rejoicing in the name of Chagville, where there are some beach facilities, parking and a children's playground. On the right is the big Convention Centre which hosts political rallies and

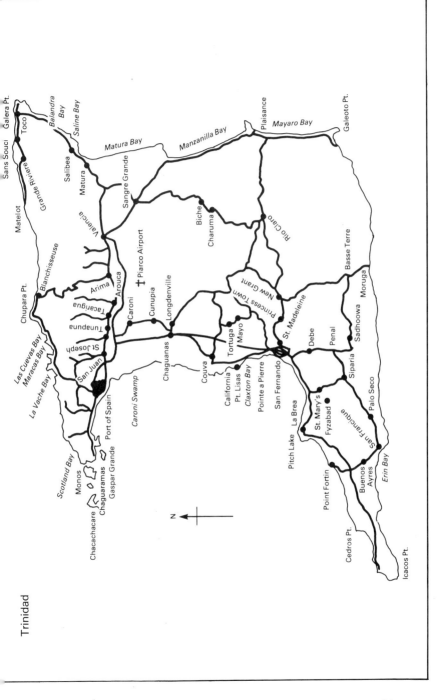

Trinidad

conventions among other things; clustered around it are the area's main developments, including the hotel school. Further along is the hangar where the Ministry of National Security houses its helicopters, and immediately afterwards comes the Yachting Association or 'Small Boats', where over 200 small yachts are based (the Trinidad Yacht Club, nearer the city, is for power boats, which are just as numerous and popular), together with the Long John Silver, a rowdy pirate boat catering for rum-sozzled floating fetes.

Half a mile further on, a turning to the left leads to a jetty where ferries make the short trip across the water to the Calypso Beach Resort on the island of Gaspar Grande; there is a small waterfront hotel there, and a small beach and beach bar, as well as holiday homes and cabanas. At Pointe Baleine, at the other end of the island, there is a cave system which has been opened up to visitors by the Tourist Board.

At the end of the road you run into another checkpoint – this one still manned, for the very tip of the peninsula is still occupied by the national coastguard and Defence Force. Here is the Chagacabana Beach Hotel, which owns a small beach – you pay for admission, and there is a basic snack bar and drinks bar. On the way back, turn left after the Convention Centre and drive towards the north coast through Tucker Valley, passing a public golf course (hidden behind trees on the left, so a pleasant surprise when you find it), and you wind up at Macqueripe Bay, a small sheltered cove down a steep flight of steps. Overlooking the bay is a derelict building which the Americans used as a club and hotel, and which is due to be revived.

On the way back into Port of Spain, branch left from the main highway into the Diego Martin valley which we saw from Fort George. It is filled from one end to the other with mostly middle-class housing and a highway runs through the middle. If you follow the old Diego Martin main road, however you pass through a string of small communities; on the left is a curious house where the leading calypsonian Lord Kitchener lives – it's called Rainorama after a 1973 calypso classic (Carnival had been delayed the previous year by a polio scare, and when it was finally held in May it was virtually washed out by rain). On the other side of the valley, on Simeon Road, is Sparrow's Hideaway, run by Kitchener's great rival the Mighty Sparrow, and where some of the best out of season calypso can be found. At the end of the valley a short walk takes you to Blue Basin, where a waterfall plunges into a deep dark pool to form a popular swimming and picnicking spot. Nearby, the Tourist Board has restored the majestic water wheel that supplied the power for River Estate, the plantation which once occupied this end of the valley. There is a small museum recalling plantation life of a century and a half ago. Finally the road climbs the steep hillside to the radio signal station at North Post, which looks out over the open sea to the north and along the steep coastline towards Maracas.

The North Coast

It has to be admitted that Trinidad does not have the Caribbean's best beaches (Tobago's are much better). You have to move a long way from the capital before you find beaches of any size or seclusion, and they don't have the gleaming white sand of the tourist brochures nor the clear still blue water – Trinidad is too close to the Orinoco estuary for that.

The best beach near Port of Spain is at Maracas Bay, 14 miles and 35 minutes' drive away. It is a mile-long curve of sand on a sheltered bay with recently upgraded facilities, but be careful of rough water and currents. The drive there is one of Trinidad's best. You leave the city on Saddle Road from the north-west corner of the Savannah, by the Hollows, and branch right at the first junction. The road heads straight for the hills, winds through the village of Maraval and past the St Andrew's golf course at Moka, then starts to twist and climb. The 'saddle' is a narrow pass through the rock where the road divides: turn left, and follow the road up and over the hills, snaking along the north coast high above the sea and beneath high forested cliffs. As you approach Maracas there is a lookout, below which is a new club and restaurant called Timberline. Then the road descends rapidly to the sea; a hotel on the western end of the beach, by the little fishing village, was nearing completion in 1985.

A few miles further on, around the headland, you come to Las Cuevas beach (the caves), which also has new Tourist Board facilities and calmer water. From there the road winds along the coast to the sleepy village of Blanchisseuse, where the water is

Maracas Beach, on Trinidad's north coast half an hour from Port of Spain

rough and the breeze strong and the beaches are normally empty; there are several unmarked beaches along the way to explore. On the far side of Blanchisseuse, across the slow dark river, the road peters out: for escapists or strong walkers there is a long, lonely and exhilarating trek along the coast to Matelot.

From Blanchisseuse you can return to Port of Spain along the most beautiful drive in Trinidad, across the northern range to Arima. It's a long twisting drive that takes you high into the hills, into that strange silent part of the forest where all you can hear is the dripping of water and the calling of birds, before descending slowly towards the central Trinidad plains past the Asa Wright Nature Centre (see Chapter 10). Take it at a leisurely pace, allowing more than half a day, stopping often to breathe cool air and listen to the silence. The road eventually joins the Eastern Main Road and the Churchill–Roosevelt Highway.

If, on the way to Maracas, you go straight on through the 'saddle' instead of turning left towards the sea, you burst suddenly into the green Santa Cruz valley, and wind through old cocoa and citrus estates between stubbled hills. This is a shorter drive through one of

The hills of the Northern Range, from the monastery at Mount St Benedict

Trinidad's loveliest valleys, but it takes you in due course straight into one of its busiest intersections, the Croisée (pronounced Kwaysay) on the Eastern Main Road at San Juan. Summoning up your patience, however, and heading east along the Eastern Main Road, you can shortly explore several other valleys reaching up into the hills of the northern range. The first (via Abercromby Street in St Joseph, just before the mosque) is Maracas Royal Road, leading through the Maracas Valley to the towering El Tucuche. The valley is the best starting point for climbing the mountain, and for a hike to the spectacular 400-foot Maracas waterfall (for directions, consult the book by Richard ffrench and Peter Bacon, *Nature Trails of Trinidad*, listed in Chapter 14.

Further up the Eastern Main Road at Tunapuna, a left turn at St John's Road will take you up Mount St Benedict, where Benedictine monks with their customary eye for a good site founded a monastery with a glorious view across the central Trinidad plain. It also has a simple but hospitable rest house, an ideal place for anyone suffering by this time from nervous strain or fatigue.

The next valley winds up the Caura River, a popular bathing and picnic spot, to a recreation park. Over the hill is the Lopinot valley: a winding, precipitous five-mile drive along the Arouca River brings you to a flat platform in the hills which is famous for its parang music. The villagers are descended from the old peons, people of mixed African, Amerindian and Spanish descent, who came from Venezuela and were largely responsible for introducing cocoa to Trinidad. Spanish and patois are still spoken. The village is named after a French count, Charles Joseph of Lopinot, who arrived in Trinidad from Santo Domingo in 1800 demanding a grant of land as a reward for fighting with the British there. His perseverance paid off, and after a false start in Arouca he marched up the narrow valley to start a cocoa plantation on this lovely flat land beneath a wall of hills. He is buried at the northern end of the village. Some of the villagers say that on dark stormy nights the old count appears on a black horse in military uniform and gallops across the old estate, sword held high, sparks flying from the horse's hoofs; he vanishes near the 'hanging tree' where another story claims he disposed of unruly slaves.

The count's house has been restored as a historic site by the Tourist Board and the grounds are landscaped. There is a small museum, and the curator can be fairly easily induced to break into some parang. Some of the villagers came to Lopinot in the 1940's from the adjoining Caura valley when the government of the day announced it would build a Caura Dam (it was never built); they brought their patron saint La Veronica across the mountains with them to the new church at Lopinot. There are caves in the limestone hills around the village, some of which are barely explored.

The East

You will have seen by now that exploring Trinidad is more a matter of travelling than arriving: of nosing around seeing what this curious island looks like and how the people are, rather than heading for specific sites and attractions. It is an island for people who are curious and relaxed, rather than for dedicated tourists with a list of sights to cover. And this is particularly true of Trinidad beyond the north-west corner with its capital and congested suburbs. The sensible thing to do is hire a car and take off, either following the general directions suggested below, or simply wandering along as the mood takes you. Peg your route to hotels if necessary, for there are not many. There is an airport hotel at Piarco airport and a pleasant guest-house at Mount St Benedict, as well as accommodation at the Asa Wright Centre, all in the general direction of Arima. There are hotels in San Fernando and nearby Claxton Bay, and guest-house accommodation at Mayaro on the east coast.

Port of Spain cheerfully assumes that north-west Trinidad *is* Trinidad, indeed Trinidad and Tobago. 'East' and 'south' begin more or less as you clear the city suburbs. Heading east, join the Churchill-Roosevelt Highway out of Port of Spain towards the airport and Arima. You pass through the second American wartime base at Wallerfield, which explains why the road is so good – the Americans built it largely for their own use. After Wallerfield it stops dead in the middle of nowhere, and you must swing left to join the older Eastern Main Road a little distance away. At Valencia, the road forks. The left-hand fork takes you to the north-east corner of Trinidad, the Toco area, while the right-hand road weaves its way down to the Atlantic coast at Manzanilla.

Toco's great charm lies in the rugged coastline which the road hugs for most of the way. This is a good two-hour drive from Port of Spain, but a useful place to stop is Balandra Bay, which has a good beach; nearby a large resort is still in the making – houses, apartments, a clubhouse and restaurant and a golf course overlooking the sea. Toco itself is a quiet village; when you get there, turn right and drive for a mile or so. You pass Salybia beach, off which is one of Trinidad's very few coral reefs, and reach an abandoned lighthouse at the very tip of the island, Galera Point. You can scramble down the rocks towards the point where Atlantic and Caribbean meet in a flurry of wind and surf: it's a special, natural place. From Toco, a road winds back along the north coast to the village of Matelot, after which you take to your feet with a tent if you want to explore the north coast further: it's a two-day walk to Blanchisseuse.

If you take the right fork at Valencia, the road heads through the market town of Sangre Grande towards the Atlantic and a drive of several miles beside the surf through acres of coconut palms. The beach is largely deserted, though there are new Tourist Board facilities at Manzanilla. Mayaro is the main settlement until you get

Balandra Beach, on Trinidad's rugged north-east coast

to the south-east tip of the island at Galeota Point and Guayaguay-are, where Amoco Trinidad brings its oil ashore. Nearby are the Trinity Hills which Columbus no doubt saw as he approached Trinidad, though they are hardly the 'three mountain peaks' beloved of the guide books. From Mayaro you can head straight across the island through Rio Claro and Princes Town to San Fernando and the 'south'.

The South

Going south means leaving the Churchill-Roosevelt Highway a few miles outside Port of Spain and turning right onto the Uriah Butler Highway. You pass the entrance to the Caroni Swamp (see Chapter 10), from where tours begin in the middle and later afternoon. At Chaguanas – where V. S. Naipaul's family lived (the house on which he based *A House for Mr Biswas* is on the main street not far from the Highway) – the road becomes the Solomon Hochoy Highway after the country's first Governor General, and heads on across the sugar plains and past Couva. The big Point Lisas industrial estate is nearby on the right, where the country's natural gas is used to produce steel and fertilizers, methanol and urea. Beyond the giant oil refinery at Pointe a Pierre is the country's second town, San Fernando: long before you get there you will see the San Fernando Hill on the horizon. Once it was a beautiful wooded hill; now it is scarred and arid from quarrying. A television commercial politely referred to the town spreading around 'the sculptured hill'.

Pitch to take away: the Pitch Lake at La Brea

San Fernando is the capital of the south and of the oil industry. It was an old Amerindian settlement – Annaparima, which may have meant 'the place without water' – but began to grow as the new French settlers of the late 18th century laid out sugar plantations, and it grew faster as the oil industry developed. Most of the oil producing fields, both on land and offshore, are in the south, and San Fernando is flanked by the two refineries at Pointe a Pierre and Point Fortin.

From San Fernando the road moves on into what Port of Spain thinks of as the 'deep south': the oil town of Point Fortin, the village of La Brea, Granville Beach and the Cedros peninsula. At La Brea, the Pitch Lake is listed as one of Trinidad's few certified tourist attractions; it is a fascinating spot, though, simply as a sight, few attractions in the world can be so wholly unappealing. The lake looks like an overgrown and deserted car park; there are new Tourist Board facilities, but also some excessively zealous and assertive guides (unofficial).

But let your imagination work a bit. The Pitch Lake is a dark mass of natural asphalt, moving imperceptibly, churning up from a depth of over 250 feet, endlessly replenishing the material which is taken out for bitumen and used on highways and mastic asphalt roofs all over the world. It is not a unique phenomenon (there is a similar lake not far away on the other side of the Gulf); but it is a rare one and not normally accessible. The cause of it is the slow seepage of crude oil or bitumen from underground reservoirs through cracks in the earth, in this case through a fault-line in the sandstone. The asphalt is a mixture of salt water, bitumen, gas and mineral matter. For some distance around, the seepage makes the surface unstable, as you can readily see from the state of the road and the tilt of the houses. The people of La Brea say the sulphurous water of the lake is healthy to bathe in.

The surface of the lake is firm enough to support people and vehicles – though not for long: a car would sink to its axles in a few hours. In the centre are several 'mothers of the lake' – slowly churning areas where soft pitch oozes and flows. A stick, stuck into one of these areas, will disappear within minutes. Since the lake is a moving mass, objects which disappear in one part of it frequently reappear somewhere else. In 1910 attempts were made to measure the depth of the pitch, but at about 150 feet the currents below began to twist and snap the cast iron pipe which was being used, bits of which surfaced for years afterwards. Tree stumps and logs regularly emerge on the surface and vanish again. Occasionally, the remains of large mammals which roamed Trinidad at the end of the last ice age have turned up in the pitch. In later times Sir Walter Raleigh patched his leaking ships with pitch from the lake, and was pleased to find it did not melt easily; the pitch has been exploited on a large or small scale by almost every administration sinc ?. The Amerindians of Trinidad – according to the historian E. L. Jo eph – believed that the Pitch Lake was created by the Good Spi it to drown a village whose people had sinned by killing too i. any hummingbirds.

This southern peninsula is best explored in a leisurely and aimless way: the south coast, the villages of Debe and Penal, Siparia and Palo Seco, Cedros and Fyzabad (scene of the fatal oilfield killings in 1937), all a far cry from the congestion of the north-west. As an alternative route back to Port of Spain, return to San Fernando but head eastwards towards Princes Town. This takes you through the rolling south Trinidad countryside, past one of the major sugar factories at Usine St Madeleine, and almost into the middle of Trinidad. A turn to the right leads to Moruga, where Columbus probably did not land, but where the landing is re-enacted anyway on August 1. Then, instead of heading across country towards Mayaro, swing northwards and meander through the woods and hills towards the central Montserrat Hills, through New Grant, Flanagin Town, and the green canefields, back to Chaguanas. There you can rejoin the Highway or use the older Southern Main Road to head back to town.

Anyone willing to leave the car behind and take to their feet and Trinidad's many nature trails should buy, beg, borrow or steal a copy of *Nature Trails of Trinidad* by Richard ffrench and Peter Bacon (SM Publications, Port of Spain, 1982). It is a slim volume giving clear, practical instructions (including maps) on 30 hikes, ranging from easy to very tough, from a half-hour stroll to a full day's trekking. It includes directions on how to climb El Tucuche, how to find the Aripo Caves (Trinidad's largest cave system with another oil-bird colony), how to reach the big reservoirs and how to hike the lonely north coast.

13

Tobago

As in Trinidad, so in Tobago: start at the top.

Behind the little capital town of Scarborough – whose name is a British fingerprint as unmistakable as a yeti's footmark – a road winds up the hill, wanders through the grounds of the island's hospital, past the sheets hanging up to dry, and emerges suddenly 430 feet above the sea in the middle of a fortress; or at least the remains of one. The polished cannon peer out across the red roofs of the town below, over the now carefully landscaped hillside and the great sweep of Rockly Bay. A tourist guide sits on the steps of the old officers' mess, waiting for business and reading the news-

Store Bay, between Crown Point and Crown Reef hotels

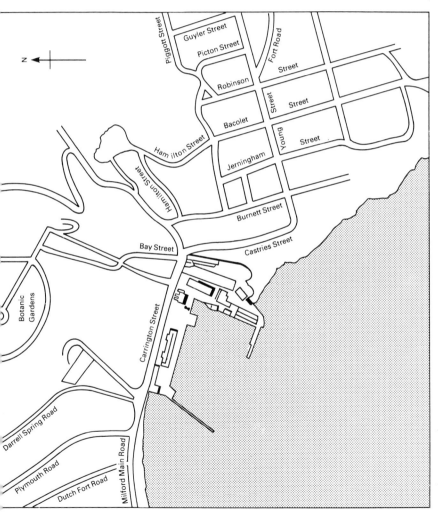

115

Tobago

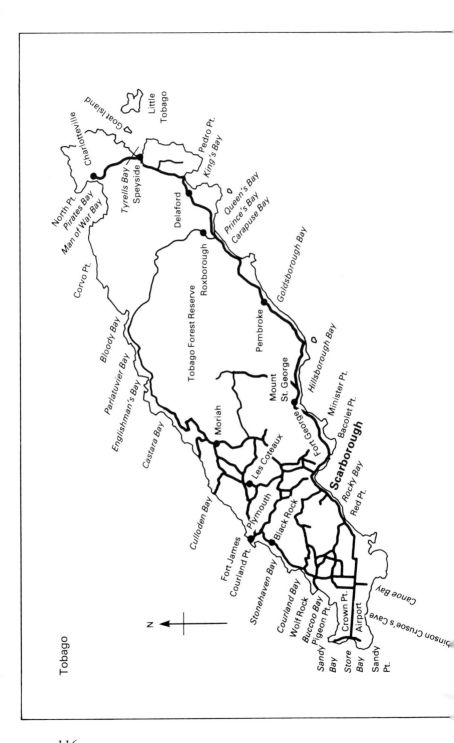

paper; a little way below, the powder magazine with its thick stone walls set into the hillside now has its ammunition rooms full of chickens and their squawking families.

From this vantage point, you can see a good deal of Tobago's lovely 116 square miles: the low, palm-covered land to the south-west, where the airport is; the central spine of hills rising to 1,900 feet in the north; the meandering Atlantic coast with its empty beaches and surf-sprayed cliffs and bays. The trade winds crackle through the ropes of the flag-mast above the fort; on the same winds, once, the westbound slavers sailed, the sugar brigantines to take off the crops, the men of war on raiding expeditions, rolling out of the dark blue surf-flecked Atlantic.

The British built Fort King George in the 1770's, in a phase of nervous fortification that produced little batteries and lookouts along much of Tobago's coast. They were trying to consolidate their hold on the island after decades of futile struggle between the European powers, though none of the new forts stopped the French taking control again soon after Fort King George was finished. Tobago's tranquil present – sold in tourist promotions as a contrast to Trinidad's vitality – is still bound up with echoes of its turbulent past.

Tobago's Crown Point airport, newly renovated, is on the south-western tip, and if you land there from Trinidad or Miami you are already near some enticing beaches. A couple of minutes from the terminal is Store Bay, nestling between Crown Point and Crown Reef Hotels; it is popular at weekends, but during the week you may find little more than a relaxed coastguard perched in his lookout, contemplating a single bather and a couple of moored fishing boats across the gently sloping sand. A little further on is Tobago's most famous beach, Pigeon Point, a long white-sand palm-shaded beach falling gently into the warm blue-green water. Pigeon Point is privately owned and there is a small entrance fee, but in return there are new beach facilities, palm-thatched shelters, a snack bar, toilets and showers, and a small shop supplying beach and diving equipment. Only the mildest hazards lurk amid this idyll: signs on the palm trees warn, 'Beware of falling nuts'.

Pigeon Point is one side of the long sweep of Buccoo Bay, across the mouth of which stretches one of the world's most accessible coral reefs, Buccoo Reef. If St Lucia has the drive-in volcano, Tobago has the cruise-in reef, for at Pigeon Point or at the village of

Tobago's most famous beach: Pigeon Point

Buccoo on the other side of the bay you can take a glass-bottomed
boat the mile or two out to the surf-line and there, besnorkelled,
slide into shallow water and the entracing world of the reef. You
don't need any snorkelling experience simply to slip on a mask and
introduce yourself to yellow angel-fish and purple damsel and blue
parrot-fish cruising the coral. What you do need, however, are
rubber slippers (usually supplied by the boats) to protect your feet
from the sharp coral, and a T-shirt to protect your back from the
sun. It's completely taboo to interfere with the marine life or
remove even a millimetre of coral; both are protected by the law,
for the reef has suffered badly from enthusiastic souvenir hunters in
years gone by. On the way back, the boats usually pause for a while
in the Nylon Pool in the middle of the bay, where the water is
unusually clear, warm and shallow.

Tobago's western coast is the calm, leeward side of the island,
where many of the beachfront hotels are. You pass them on the way
up the coast, as well as the 125-acre, 18-hole, palm-shaded golf
course next to the Mount Irvine Hotel (where there is also a small
Museum of Tobago History). Between Mount Irvine and the village

of Black Rock lies the Grafton Estate, one of Tobago's attractions for birdwatchers (see Chapter 10). The estate is a former plantation that was devastated, as most of the island was, by a hurricane called Flora in 1963, and has since largely reverted to wilderness, a situation apparently welcomed by the birds.

The little town of Plymouth is the main centre on this leeward coast, and it has little of the bustling activity of the British naval port which shares its name. It nestles at the northern end of the great sweep of Courland Bay, the near-empty beach whose name is a reminder of the Courlanders who settled the area; another old British fort, Fort James, commands the headland and the bay. There is not much left of Fort James, but again the site is carefully landscaped. Just below – take the first road to the right after leaving the Fort – is a promontory, the site of some of the earliest settlements in Tobago. A modern monument, unveiled in 1978, is by the sculptor Janis Mintiks and is dedicated to 'the bold, enterprising and industrious Courlanders from faraway Latvia on the Baltic shore, who lived in this area, named after them, from 1639 to 1693.'

Back on the main road, you are near a curious tomb whose inscription has intrigued generations of Tobagonians and visitors. It

Fish vendor, Charlotteville, Tobago

is the 1783 grave of young Betty Stiven and her baby, and the inscription states that 'what was remarkable of her' was that 'she was a mother without knowing it, and a wife without letting her husband know it, except by her kind indulgence to him'. The stone was placed by her husband, who records that 'to the end of his days (he) will deplore her death'. Presumably this means that poor Betty died in childbirth and her child with her or soon after, and that she had been such a tactful, discreet and sensitive wife that her fortunate husband Alexander had no cause to remember the common burdens of wedlock. No wonder he deplored her loss.

Further up the coast you pass the Arnos Vale Hotel, a favourite centre for naturalists, and a few miles further on Britain's 'royal photographer' Norman Parkinson, a Tobagonian by adoption, has made his home, a beautiful clifftop house from where he sallies forth on international assignments. Parkinson is a much liked and respected resident, who for a while also manufactured pork sausages as a sideline, marketing them as Famous Porkinson Bangers; but don't disturb him.

Once, you could follow the road all the way up the western coast to the northern tip and Charlotteville, but no more – at least unless you have a sturdy four-wheel-drive vehicle and a lot of patience.

Scarborough, Tobago's capital, has a lively market and something Port of Spain sorely lacks – an open waterfront, so you can walk along the wave-splashed sea wall near the point where the Trinidad ferry docks, then up into the town. The road to Fort King George is on the left soon after you strike out on the Bacolet Road which heads for Roxborough and Charlotteville up the windward, Atlantic coast, clinging to the hillsides or dropping down to run for a while alongside palm-fenced beaches, often empty except for the ocean breakers. It's a narrow road full of sudden sharp bends, needing a degree of patience and caution from drivers. The real attraction is the coastline itself and the endless series of vistas it opens up of white-flecked Atlantic blue.

Beyond the village of Roxborough, about 45 minutes from Scarborough, the road heads for King's Bay with its lovely inland waterfall, Bateaux Bay with its first-rate snorkelling, and the fishing village of Speyside; then it drops suddenly towards the natural harbour of Man o' War Bay and the village of Charlotteville. Speyside is the point of departure for Little Tobago (see Chapter 10) where, even if there are no Birds of Paradise, there is a well-kept nature reserve which is a major nesting centre for sea-birds.

Puzzles

Some intriguing research is going on which could shed some light on Tobago's geological past. While Trinidad is known to have been part of the South American continent, and it is assumed that Tobago was too at a much more distant time (Tobago is 21 miles from Trinidad, while Trinidad is only seven from Venezuela), recent studies have shown that certain species of frogs, lizards, birds and snakes found in Tobago are strikingly similar to species in parts of the South American mainland, but are unknown in Trinidad. Did they arrive in Tobago by sea, mysteriously by-passing the larger island, or across some ancient and long-vanished land bridge?

Another Tobago puzzle concerns the island's name. There is some sort of link with the word tobacco. Dr Williams, whose narrative proceeds at great speed, notes simply that after Columbus passed by and failed to land, Tobago remained 'virtually isolated and undiscovered . . . an Amerindian island . . . retaining its name Tobaco (whence the corruption Tobago), signifying the importance of tobacco in the Amerindian economy.' For more than two centuries, various writers have linked Tobago with the pipe used by Amerindians to smoke tobacco, which they inhaled through the nostrils, causing themselves to become 'drunk with the Fumes of it, (so) the dreams they had were in some sort inspired', according to an anonymous work of 1749, which insists that Columbus thought the silhouette of Tobago looked like the Y-shape of the Amerindian pipe.

That makes a nice story; but Columbus, if he sighted Tobago at all, did so only on the far distant horizon from the area of the Dragon's Mouth, an improbable feat in itself, since the tip of Tobago is 50 miles away, though Las Casas insists that from there he saw 'very high land' some 26 miles to the north-east and called it Bellaforma 'because it looked very well from a distance'. But it seems likely that Tobago was named after tobacco, not the other way around, and not after anybody's pipe. In Cuba, Columbus found Amerindians smoking rolls of dry leaves which they called tabacos: 'lighted at one end, the roll is chewed, and the smoke

Pulling in the seine at Courland Bay

inhaled at the other. It has the effect of making them sleepy and almost intoxicated, and in using it they do not feel tired'. Perhaps the early settlers named Tobago after its inhabitants' prototype cigarettes.

A third puzzle is the whole business of Robinson Crusoe. Tobago is often referred to as Robinson Crusoe's island, the island which Daniel Defoe is supposed to have had in mind when he wrote his great castaway novel *Robinson Crusoe*, published in 1719. Near Crown Point airport there is a cave in the cliffs called Robinson Crusoe's Cave, though it is hard to find and enter, which suggests that the fictional Crusoe had more alacrity than his latter-day pursuers. It is hard to escape Crusoe in Tobago; the most famous hotel of days gone by, on the hillside outside Scarborough, was named after Defoe's hero. What with Crusoe Motors, Crusoe's Grotto (a pizza house), Crusoe Chalet, Crusoe Batteries and Crusoe Condotel, not to mention the island's most famous calypsonian Tobago Crusoe, you would think Crusoe was a great nationalist hero. The story goes (apocryphally no doubt) that when one of the many Robinson Crusoe films was being shot in Tobago, one elderly observer announced that he remembered Robinson personally.

In Defoe's time there was a rash of castaway stories, one of the most dramatic being a true tale – the marooning of a sailor called Alexander Selkirk after a quarrel with his captain. He was left alone for four and a half years on the island of Mas a Tierra, in the Juan Fernandez group in the Pacific, off the coast of Chile. Selkirk was finally rescued and made much of his adventure, and there is some evidence that Defoe met him and used his story as a peg on which to hand the much more profound tale of castaway Crusoe and his black co-opted servant Man Friday.

Defoe's story digs deep into the colonial process and the problem of acculturation, and has been retold in modern times by several writers, all of whom take belated revenge by giving Friday the upper hand: Adrian Mitchell (*Man Friday*), Michel Tournier (*Friday, or The Other Island*). Derek Walcott cunningly reworked the story in his play *Pantomime*, making Crusoe the owner of a run-down Tobago guest-house and Friday his waiter and handyman.

Defoe may have scanned the maps of the Indies for a more plausible and familiar setting for his tale than far-off Mas a Tierra. He was interested in maps and travel and the sea, and there are striking parallels between Crusoe's island and Tobago. The novel's title page speaks of Crusoe living 'Eight and Twenty years all alone in an uninhabited Island on the coast of America, near the mouth of the great Orinooque . . .' That is seven times the length of Selkirk's exile, but Tobago is not far from the Orinoco delta and, as it happens, is roughly the same shape as Mas a Tierra and twice the size. Defoe is careful not to mention a name for the island, but clearly imagined it in the general area of Trinidad and Tobago.

But, unfortunately for the advocates of Crusoe, the theory cannot hold water. Defoe's hero can observe 'the great island Trinidad' lying 'to the W and N. W.' fifteen to twenty leagues away, and calculates his own latitude as 9 degrees 22 minutes north. That clearly makes Crusoe's island an imaginary one well to the south-east of Trinidad, in the opposite direction from Tobago, and close to the mouth of the Orinoco.

But mere facts are unlikely to banish the vision of Crusoe clambering over the Crown Point cliffs and encountering an amiable Tobagonian to instruct in his English ways and needs. Crusoe himself, after all, became something of a specialist in the matter of masquerades.

14

Checklist

Arrival and Departure

Piarco International Airport is about 13 miles from Port of Spain on a normally congested highway. Allow at least an hour for the trip, more if travelling to Piarco in the afternoon rush hour. For entry, you need a passport which is valid for six months beyond your stay, and a completed immigration card – keep the duplicate for departure. Extensions of landing time are possible, but ask for the maximum time on arrival. You may be asked to show a return ticket. A work permit has to be obtained in advance if you plan to do any paid work.

Airport procedures tend to be slow on arrival, but there is a green ('nothing to declare') customs line which saves going through the Customs Hall. The main airport concourse has a bank – keep your receipt if you want to change local currency back at the end of a trip – and car rental outlets, though it is wise to book a car in advance. A minibus service run by Auto Rentals leaves every half hour for most of the day, calling at major Port of Spain hotels on the way to its downtown terminal on the corner of Richmond Street and Tragarete Road. The $17 fare is well below the taxi fare of $50–60 (if taking a taxi, check the rates on the board as you leave the arrivals terminal). There is also a public bus service to Tunapuna where you can change for an express bus into downtown Port of Spain. On departure, there is an airport tax of $20 (all figures in Trinidad and Tobago currency).

Time

Local time is four hours behind GMT and one hour ahead of EST, so when it is midday in Port of Spain, it is 11 a.m. in New York and Miami, and 4 p.m. in London. During daylight saving periods, GMT and EST move ahead one hour. Trinidad and Tobago does not operate daylight saving time.

Office hours are normally 0800 to 1630 Monday to Friday, with lunch from 1200 to 1300. Stores open on Saturday mornings, and those in the malls tend to stay open late.

Money

The Trinidad and Tobago dollar is pegged to the American dollar at a rate of 3.60, so that TT$1.00 is worth just under US$0.28. Exchange rates against other currencies, including sterling, thus vary. Most commercial banks – there are eight, with 112 branches – are open from 0900 to 1400 Monday to Thursday, and 0900 to 1200 and 1500 to 1700 on Friday. Credit cards are gaining ground and are widely accepted at hotels and major stores and restaurants. American currency is not officially negotiable.

Business

The government officially encourages private sector development through fiscal and other incentives, and foreign investment is actively sought, particularly where it involves a significant transfer of technology and skills and access to export markets. Investment incentives include exemptions on import duty and income tax, export allowances, depreciation allowances, repatriation of profits, the possibility of import restrictions to protect local manufacturing, land and factory shells, and additional inducements for hotel investment. The supporting institutions include the Industrial Development Corporation (which will supply the details), the Export Development Corporation, the Development Finance Company, the Agricultural Development Bank, the Management Development Centre and the Caribbean Industrial Research Institute (CARIRI).

There is public sector participation in many areas, including agriculture and fishing, banking, oil and manufacturing, transport and communications, storage, hotels and tourism; the government owns the public utilities. Government shareholding is due to be divested to the public in due course. While key economic sectors remain as a matter of policy in the hands of nationals, and there have been successful localisation programmes in (for example) banking and insurance, joint ventures with foreign investors are encouraged. Licences under the Aliens (Landholding) Act are necessary for foreigners to buy land.

There is a Stock Exchange, a Unit Trust and a Merchant Bank. Income tax ranges up to 70 per cent for chargeable incomes over TT$60,000; corporation tax is charged at 45 per cent, and there is a 5 per cent Unemployment Levy (which is also paid by individuals with a chargeable income of over $35,000). The tax structure is under review.

Air Links

The national carrier, BWIA, flies into Port of Spain from Miami, New York, Boston, Toronto, London, Frankfurt, Zurich and Caracas, and from the following Caribbean locations: Jamaica, Puerto Rico, St Kitts, Antigua, St Lucia, St Maarten, Barbados, Grenada, Curacao, Martinique and Guyana. It operates an airbridge service to Tobago, with a return fate of $75. Other carriers flying into Piarco include British Airways, Pan Am, American, Eastern, KLM, ALM, Guyana Airways, Aeropostal, Cubana and Air Canada.

Tourist Board Offices

Trinidad: 122–124 Frederick Street, Port of Spain (627–5461, 623–4705).
Tobago: Scarborough (639–2125).
Piarco airport: airport concourse (664–5196).
New York: Suite 712–14, 400 Madison Avenue, New York 10017 (212–838–7750/1).
Miami: Suite 702, 200 Southeast First Street, Miami, Fl. 33131 (305–371 2056).
Toronto: York Centre, 145 King St. West and University Avenue, Toronto M5H 1J8 (416–367–0390).

London: 20 Lower Regent Street, London SW1Y 4PH (01–839–7155).

The Tourist Board publishes a monthly brochure on current events, which at Carnival time includes addresses of calypso tents, pan-yards and mas' camps.

Getting around

In addition to the public bus service – which has a priority route from Port of Spain through the eastern suburbs on the old railway track – there is a system of privately operated taxis, mini-buses and small buses (known as maxi-taxis). These work regular routes, dropping and picking up passengers along the way, and are the best way of getting around (there is the added advantage of information, gossip and jokes from the other passengers). Just hail one firmly by the roadside. All taxis bear licence plates starting with H, and maxi-taxis are quickly recognisable by their bright coloured stripe. Private taxis are widely available, especially at hotels, but will be expensive on long runs; they are not metered, so agree the fare in advance.

Maxi-taxis on Independence Square

To drive yourself, you need a local driving permit or an international driving permit. Vehicles are normally right-hand-drive, and drive on the left, British-style. Gas stations normally close at 9 p.m. and on Sundays. Several auto rental and tour companies are listed in the telephone directory.

Tobago

Apart from the BWIA airbridge, there are ferries sailing daily from Port of Spain and Scarborough. They can take cars. The trip takes about five hours.

Shopping

Trinidad and Tobago is not a duty free port, but a duty free system operates through certain stores, including several on lower Frederick Street, whereby duty free purchases can be made by bona fide visitors and picked up at the airport on departure. The best known stores are gathered on the lower end of Frederick Street, near Independence Square – Stecher's and Y. de Lima (for jewellery, watches, cameras, etc.), Stephens and Johnsons' department store. Most of the hotels have some shops available, and there are several shopping malls – on Long Circular Road in St James, at Westmoorings (West Mall) near St James, Trincity near the airport, Valpark, Chaguanas and San Fernando (Gulf City). Many guidebooks still suggest bargaining as a routine strategy, but have obviously not shopped recently in Trinidad and Tobago. One area little noticed by most guide books is the range of Indian goods – clothes, ornaments, furnishings. Explore the downtown area between Frederick and Charlotte Streets particularly.

Tipping

Normally 10 per cent is added to bills as a service charge. Hotels charge a 3 per cent room tax. But nobody is likely to refuse a tip.

Contacts

The telephone system has improved dramatically in recent years. There is international direct dialling, and public telephones in working order are easier to find. Telex and overseas call facilities are available at Textel on Independence Square, and there is an overseas call centre at 54 Frederick Street. Post Offices do not open on Saturdays; the main Post Office is on Wrightson Road opposite the Holiday Inn.

Climate

Trinidad tends to be a couple of degrees hotter and stickier than Tobago. Maximum day temperatures rarely exceed 33 degrees centigrade (at least at the meteorological station at Piarco), and fall to the mid or lower twenties at night. The coolest time is from Christmas to Carnival; the rainy season normally lasts from late May to December, with March and April the driest months.

Current

115 and 230 volts, 60 cycles AC.

Population

1.15 million (estimate) in 1983, of which 59,800 were in Port of Spain, 36,000 in San Fernando and 26,200 in Arima. Greater Port of Spain, including the suburbs stretching from Carenage in the west to Trincity in the east, had a population of 148,000 in 1980 and is expected to grow to 176,000 by 2000. GNP per capita: US$7,300.

Size

Trinidad 50 miles by 37, Tobago 26 miles by 7.

Long Circular Mall, at St James outside Port of Spain

Hotels

Trinidad:

Hilton Hotel, Lady Young Rd., Belmont (624–3211, 3111).
Overlooks the Savannah and the city about a mile from downtown
Port of Spain.

Holiday Inn, Wrightson Rd., Port of Spain (625–3361, 4531–8). Close to port and downtown area.

Queen's Park Hotel, Queen's Park West, Port of Spain (625–1061, 1066). Overlooks the Savannah.

Chagacabana Hotel, Western Main Road, Chaguaramas (625–1021). On a small beach half an hour from Port of Spain.

Chaconia Inn, Saddle Road, Maraval (629–2101/3, 2354). In the Maraval valley 15 minutes from Port of Spain.

Kapok Hotel, 16–18 Cotton Hill, Port of Spain (622-6441/4). Near the Savannah on Saddle Rd.

Bel Air Hotel, Piarco International Airport (664–4771/3). Near airport terminals.

Farrell House Hotel, Claxton Bay (659–2271/2).   Newly refurbished, 15 minutes north of San Fernando.

Calypso Beach Resort, Gaspar Grande (623–4803). Overlooking harbour of offshore beach resort.

Hotel Normandie, 10 Nook Avenue, St Ann's, Port of Spain (624–1181/6). Near Savannah and Queen's Hall.

Errol J. Lau Hotel, 66 Edward St., Port of Spain (625-4381/3). On the edge of the downtown area.

Monique's Guest House, 114 Saddle Rd., Maraval (629–2233). In Maraval valley just beyond Chaconia Inn.

Royal Hotel, 45–54 Royal Rd., San Fernando (652–3924). On the edge of central San Fernando.

Tobago:

Arnos Vale Hotel, Arnos Vale Estate (639–2881).

Blue Haven Hotel, Bacolet Street (639–2566).

Crown Reef Hotel, Store Bay (639–8571/6).

Coral Reef Guest House, Allfields Rd. (639–2536).

Mount Irvine Bay Hotel, Mt. Irvine (639–8871/3).

Sandy Point Beach Club, Sandy Point (639–8533/4).

Tropikist Beach Hotel, Crown Point (639–2851/2).

Turtle Beach Hotel, Courland Bay (639–2851).

Crown Point on the Bay, Crown Point (639–8781, 8784).

Cocrico Inn, North and Commissioner Streets, Plymouth (639–2961).

Della Mira Guest House, Bacolet St. (639–2531, 2239).

Kariwak Village Hotel, Store Bay Rd., Crown Point (639–8545).

Treasure Isle Hotel, Bacolet Street (639–2673, 2955).
Blue Waters Inn, Batteaux Bay, Speyside (639–4341).
Man o' War Bay Holiday Cottages, Charlotteville Estate (639–4327, 2137).

Restaurants

Trinidad:

La Boucan and Pool Terrace, Hilton Hotel, Port of Spain.
La Ronde, Holiday Inn, Port of Spain.
Mangal's Indian Restaurant, 13 Queen's Park East, Port of Spain.
Pelican Inn, 2–4 Coblentz Avenue, Port of Spain.
New Shay Shay Tien, 81 Cipriani Boulevard, Port of Spain.
Tiki Village, Kapok Hotel, Port of Spain.
Cafe Savanna, Kapok Hotel, Port of Spain.
Mango Tree, Chancery Lane, Port of Spain.
Chez Veronique, 117A, Henry Street, Port of Spain.
Veni Mange, Lucknow Street, St. James.
Chaconia Inn, Saddle Rd., Maraval.
JB's, Valpark Shopping Plaza.
The Outhouse, 82B Woodford Street, Newtown, Port of Spain.
Fisherman's Wharf, Long Circular Mall, St James.
Copper Kettle Grille, 66–68 Edward St., Port of Spain.
The Fortress, Kirpalani Plaza, Barataria.
Gallagher's Restaurant, Colsort Place, Frederick St., Port of Spain.
Soong's Great Wall Restaurant, 97 Circular Rd., San Fernando.
Il Giardino, Nook Avenue, St Ann's, Port of Spain.
The Rig, Gulf City, La Romain.
The Waterfront Restaurant, West Mall, Westmoorings.
The Verandah, 16 Gray St., St Clair, Port of Spain.
Villa Creole, 133 Western Main Rd., St James.
Char-B-Que, Maraval and Tragarete Roads, Port of Spain.

Tobago:

Blue Haven Hotel, Bacolet St.
Cocrico Inn, North and Commissioner Sts., Plymouth.
Crown Reef Hotel, Store Bay.

Mt. Irvine Bay Hotel, Mt. Irvine.
Old Donkey Cart, Bacolet St.
The Steak Hut, Sandy Point Beach Club, Sandy Point.
Tropikist Beach Hotel, Crown Point.
Turtle Beach Hotel, Courland Bay.
Kariwak Village Hotel, Store Bay Rd., Crown Point.
Voodoo Nest, Main and Bacolet Sts., Scarborough.
Mon Cheri, Grafton Rd., Black Rock.

For Further Reading

There are personal views of Trinidad in V. S. Naipaul's acerbic *The Middle Passage* (Penguin, 1969) and Patrick Leigh Fermor's *The Traveller's Tree* (1950, republished by Penguin in 1984). *David Frost introduces Trinidad and Tobago* (Deutsch, 1975), edited by Michael Anthony and Andrew Carr, is a collection of chapters by different writers on specific areas of national life.

Dr. Eric Williams wrote a *History of the People of Trinidad and Tobago* in a month as an independence gift to the population (PNM Publishing Co., Port of Spain, 1962, republished by Deutsch), and covered the whole Caribbean in *From Columbus to Castro* (Deutsch, 1970). Bridget Brereton's *A History of Modern Trinidad 1783–1962*, (Heinemann, 1981) is a major, more recent study. The novelist Michael Anthony has also turned to history and his two-volume *The Making of Port of Spain* (Port of Spain, 1978, 1983) accommodates both broad background material and specific details of daily life; among his other works are *Glimpses of Trinidad and Tobago* (Columbus Publishers, Port of Spain, 1974) and *Profile Trinidad* (Macmillan, 1982) which traces the Trinidad story up to 1900. John La Guerre has assembled a useful collection of studies on the Indian presence in Trinidad in *From Calcutta to Caroni – The East Indians of Trinidad* (Longman, 1974). Fr Anthony de Verteuil's *The Years Before* is a close-up of Trinidad in the years immediately before emancipation (Inprint Caribbean, Port of Spain, 1981), while Olga Mavrogordato's *Voices in the Street*, also from Inprint (1977), is a series of historical vignettes.

The indispensible book on Carnival is Errol Hill's *The Trinidad Carnival – Mandate for a National Theatre* (University of Texas, 1972), while John Newel Lewis's memories and sketches from the judges' table in *Nobody in his Right Mind* (Interworld Selections, Thornhill, Canada, 1979) gives a feel of what it's like to be in the middle of it all. For calypso, the main works are Keith Warner's *The Trinidad Calypso* (Heinemann, 1983) and *Atilla's Kaiso* by Atilla the Hun (Raymond Quevedo) (Trinidad, 1983).

For fiction, much of the best work has come from V. S. Naipaul (*The Mystic Masseur, The Suffrage of Elvira, Miguel Street, A House for Mr Biswas, Guerrillas, The Mimic Men*), though his critical approach to his native land has somewhat tempered the popularity he might have enjoyed there. There is an affectionate memoir in *Finding the Centre*, however (Deutsch, 1984), and Naipaul's venture into Trinidad history – *The Loss of El Dorado* – is a novelist's exploration of some dark and intriguing historical shadows. Other major novelists are Earl Lovelace (*The Schoolmaster, The Dragon Can't Dance, The Wine of Astonishment*) and Samuel Selvon (*The Lonely Londoners, A Brighter Sun, The Plains of Caroni*). Shiva Naipaul's first two novels (*Fireflies* and *The Chip-Chip Gatherers*) are set affectionately in Trinidad. Look too for C. L. R. James's *Minty Alley*, Ralph de Boissiere's *Crown Jewel* and Merle Hodge's *Crick Crack Monkey*. Poetry and drama are dominated by Derek Walcott, and the major writer in dialect is Paul Keens-Douglas.

There are several books of reminiscence which give a feel of the society in recent years. Among them are Albert Gomes's *Through a Maze of Colour* (Key Caribbean, Port of Spain, 1974), Dr Winston Mahabir's *In and Out of Politics* (Inprint Caribbean, 1978), Dr Patrick Solomon's *Solomon – an autobiography* (Inprint, 1981), Dr Eric Williams's *Inward Hunger – the Education of a Prime Minister* (Deutsch, 1969) and P. E. T. O'Connor's *Some Trinidad Yesterdays* (Inprint, 1978). Dr Selwyn Ryan's *Race and Nationalism in Trinidad and Tobago* (University of Toronto, 1972) covers political history from 1919 to the early seventies.

Molly Ahye's *Golden Heritage – the Dance in Trinidad and Tobago* (Port of Spain, 1978) was followed by *Cradle of Caribbean Dance* in 1983, a study of Beryl McBurnie and her pioneering work with the Little Carib Theatre. The National Cultural Council published in 1977 Daphne Pawan Taylor's study, *Parang of Trinidad*, while the Lopinot story is explored in Archibald Chauharjasingh's *Lopinot in History* (Port of Spain, 1982). John Newel Lewis's *Ajoupa* (Port of Spain, 1983) deals with Trinidad's architecture, as does in a collection of drawings – Gerald Watterson's *This Old House* (Paria

Publishing Co., Port of Spain, 1983).

In addition to *Nature Trails of Trinidad*, referred to in Chapter 12, the naturalist will need Richard ffrench's *A Guide to the Birds of Trinidad and Tobago* (Harrowood Books, 1976), the standard reference work.